BATMAN THE KILLING JOKE

THE DELUXE EDITION

Dan DiDio Senior VP-Executive Editor
Denny O'Neil, Mark Chiarello Editors- original title
Bob Harras Editor-collected edition
Robbin Brosterman Senior Art Director
Louis Prandi Art Director
Paul Levitz President & Publisher
Georg Brewer VP-Design & DC Direct Creative
Richard Bruning Senior VP-Creative Director
Patrick Caldon Executive VP-Finance & Operations
Chris Caramalis VP-Finance
John Cunningham VP-Marketing
Terri Cunningham VP-Managing Editor
Alison Gill VP-Manufacturing
David Hyde VP-Publicity
Hank Kanalz VP-General Manager, WildStorm
Jim Lee Editorial Director-WildStorm
Paula Lowitt Senior VP-Business & Legal Affairs
MaryEllen McLaughlin VP-Advertising & Custom Publishing
John Nee Senior VP-Business Development
Gregory Noveck Senior VP-Creative Affairs
Sue Pohja VP-Book Trade Sales
Steve Rotterdam Senior VP -Sales & Marketing
Cheryl Rubin Senior VP-Brand Management
Jeff Trojan VP-Business Development, DC Direct
Bob Wayne VP-Sales

Cover by **Brian Bolland**

Batman: The Killing Joke: The Deluxe Edition
ISBN-13: 9781845767723

Published by Titan Books, a division of Titan Publishing Group Ltd.
144 Southwark Street, London SE1 0UP.

Printed in Spain.
First published: April 2008
7 8 9 10

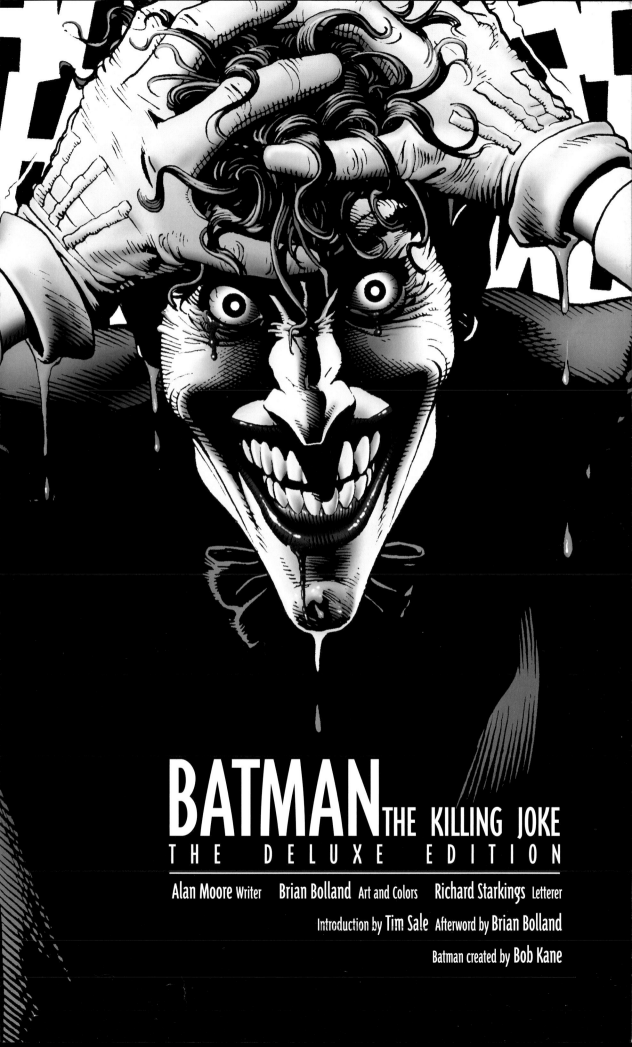

BATMAN THE KILLING JOKE
THE DELUXE EDITION

Alan Moore Writer   **Brian Bolland** Art and Colors   **Richard Starkings** Letterer

Introduction by **Tim Sale**   Afterword by **Brian Bolland**

Batman created by **Bob Kane**

INTRODUCTION

Man, how cool is this?

Like everyone who was in the mainstream comics field in the late 1980s, or — as was my case — had their noses pressed against the glass, the back-to-back-to-back-to-back of DARK KNIGHT RETURNS, WATCHMEN, BATMAN: YEAR ONE, and BATMAN: THE KILLING JOKE, completely reenergized the field. The characters (other than those in WATCHMEN) had been around for decades and, while many talented writers and artists had done much notable work in that time, there was an incredible sense of the new coming from Frank Miller and this handful of crazy Brits — Alan Moore, Brian Bolland, John Higgins, Richard Starkings and Dave Gibbons — who were seeing possibilities in them, in the kinds of stories that could be told, and not incidentally, in the way that a story could be presented.

BATMAN: THE KILLING JOKE is the only one of the stories listed above that did not first exist in another format, as a series of comics that were eventually collected into that catch-all term, a "graphic novel." THE KILLING JOKE was a 46-page story, but it was crafted at such an astonishing level, and printed so much more cleanly and carefully, that it seemed to be a different beast altogether, not just a really great Batman comic, but something different. I didn't get it then, but I do now.

That is what authors of extraordinary craft can do: make the old seem new.

And thrilling. Don't forget thrilling.

I am told that the origins of BATMAN: THE KILLING JOKE go back to a Batman/Judge Dredd proposal that Moore and Bolland had cooked up. When it fell through, Moore asked Bolland what else he wanted to do, and Bolland said, "The Joker, please."

So polite. And thus a classic was born.

Moore is famous for many things, not the least of which are his maniacally controlled and precisely orchestrated scripts, requiring an equal and similar effort from his artist partner, and in the amazing Brian Bolland he found an artist his equal in talent, fanaticism, care, and expressiveness. Both excel in impressing with their rendering of the mundane, so that it never *feels* mundane. And then they blast into a reveal, a money shot so explosive that is it only then that you realize how well you, as a reader, have been lulled to rest *on purpose*, just to set you up.

The Joker's reveal on page 11, the tragic event on page 18, the second reveal on page 37, all orchestrated and carried out in ways that astonish, and then astonish again when you go back and see just how much these artists have known and set things up from the beginning. How fun it is to be in the hands of creators who know so much about what they are doing.

Oh, and the joke (how cool is it that the book ends with a joke) at the finish?

Priceless, funny, and perfect for the characters of Batman and The Joker.

What you hold in your hands, though, is not the book that I own, that so inflamed(!) me and thousands of others back in 1988, because of one crucial element: the coloring.

This time around, you lucky buggers, you have the fantastic treat to see the book colored by the artist himself, and see his more complete vision of how the story should look. Side by side, the comparison is amazing.

Bolland's colors are characteristically thoughtful and restrained. They fit the work more completely than Higgins's state-of-the-art job in 1988 and are a joy to look at. Slow down and one can see how cool the palette is now, versus the warmer one of 1988, and how much better that reflects the somber tone of the story, and how, when Bolland retains a color from 1988 that has become iconic, like Barbara's yellow shirt, he integrates that so well into the cooler colors in the scene, allowing the shirt to really pop and ratchet up the horror of the event.

But the biggest and most amazing change in this newly colored edition is in the flashback sequences.

Bolland washes out all color in each one, but chooses to spotlight an object in each — a bowl of tentacles, shrimp, and so on — in increasingly

intense shades of red, all leading up to (here's that sense that everything has been planned from the start by masterful hands) the Red Hood that was posited to be The Joker's mostly forgotten origin, *way back in 1951,* and the transformation of the milquetoast failed comedian to insane criminal mastermind.

Brrrrrr. I just got chills.

Anyone else get chills?

Man, how cool is this?

Tim Sale

Pasadena, CA 2008

Tim Sale lives in southern California with his aged dogs Hotspur and Shelby. Raised in Seattle, he still finds California an odd place, though he hopes that will change someday.

Tim is the artist on BATMAN: DARK VICTORY, CATWOMAN: WHEN IN ROME, BATMAN: THE LONG HALLOWEEN and many other titles.

In 2006, Tim became the artist for the hit NBC television series Heroes.

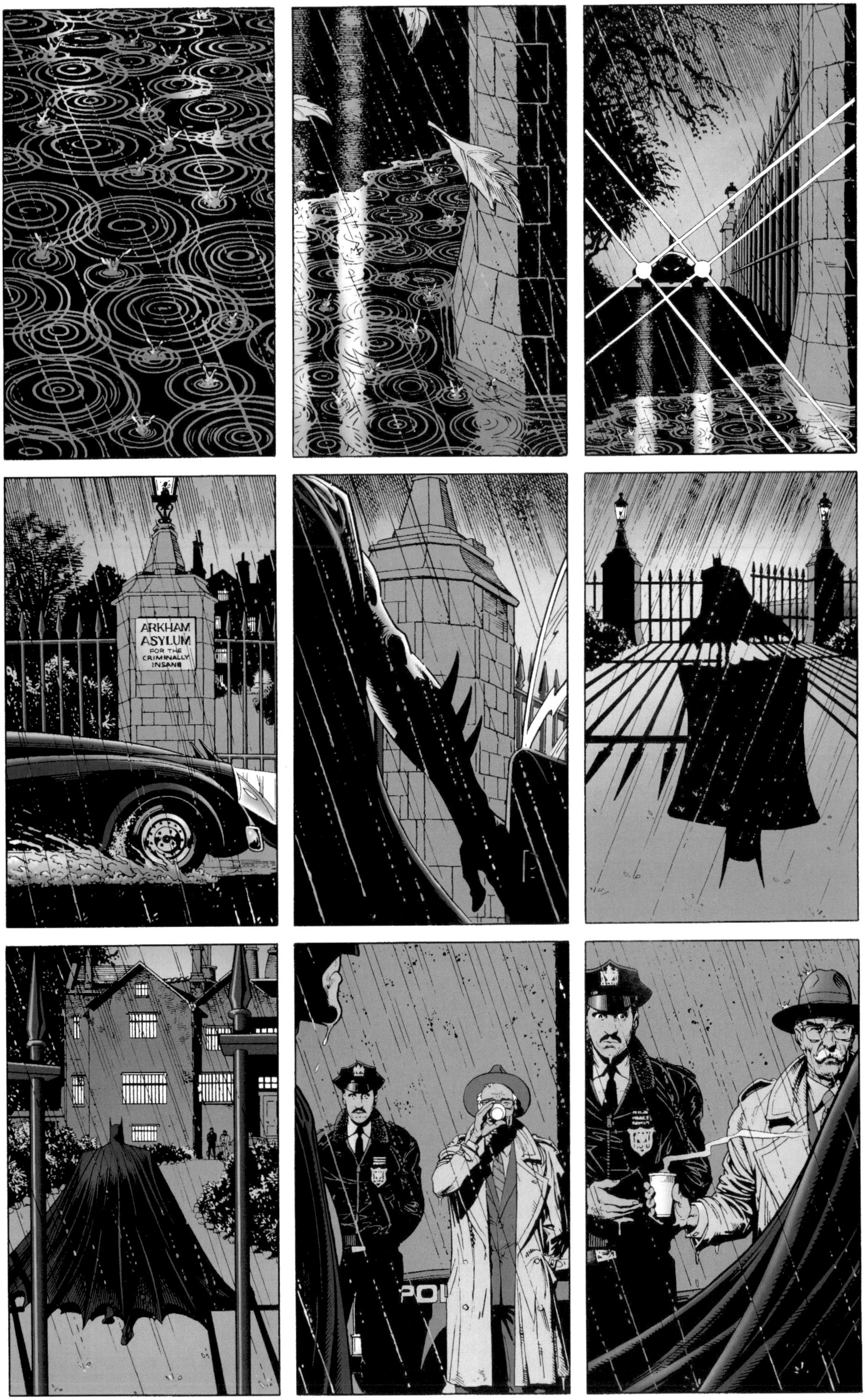
ARKHAM
ASYLUM
FOR THE
CRIMINALLY
INSANE

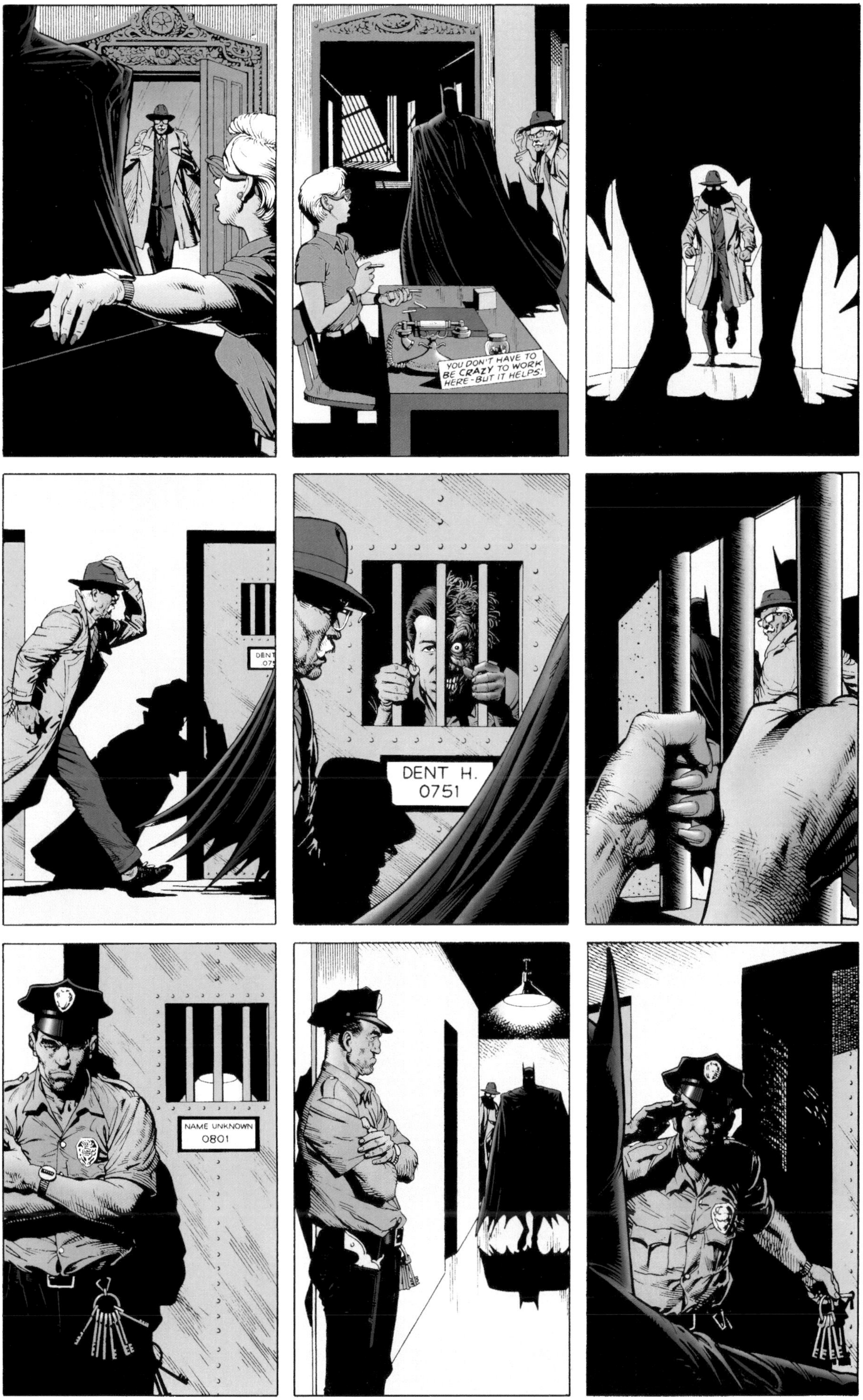
YOU DON'T HAVE TO BE CRAZY TO WORK HERE-BUT IT HELPS!
DENT H.
0751
NAME UNKNOWN
0801

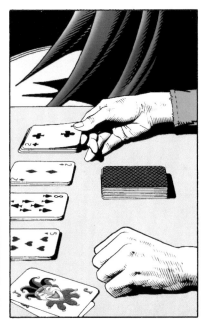

THERE WERE THESE TWO
GUYS IN A LUNATIC
ASYLUM...

FNAP

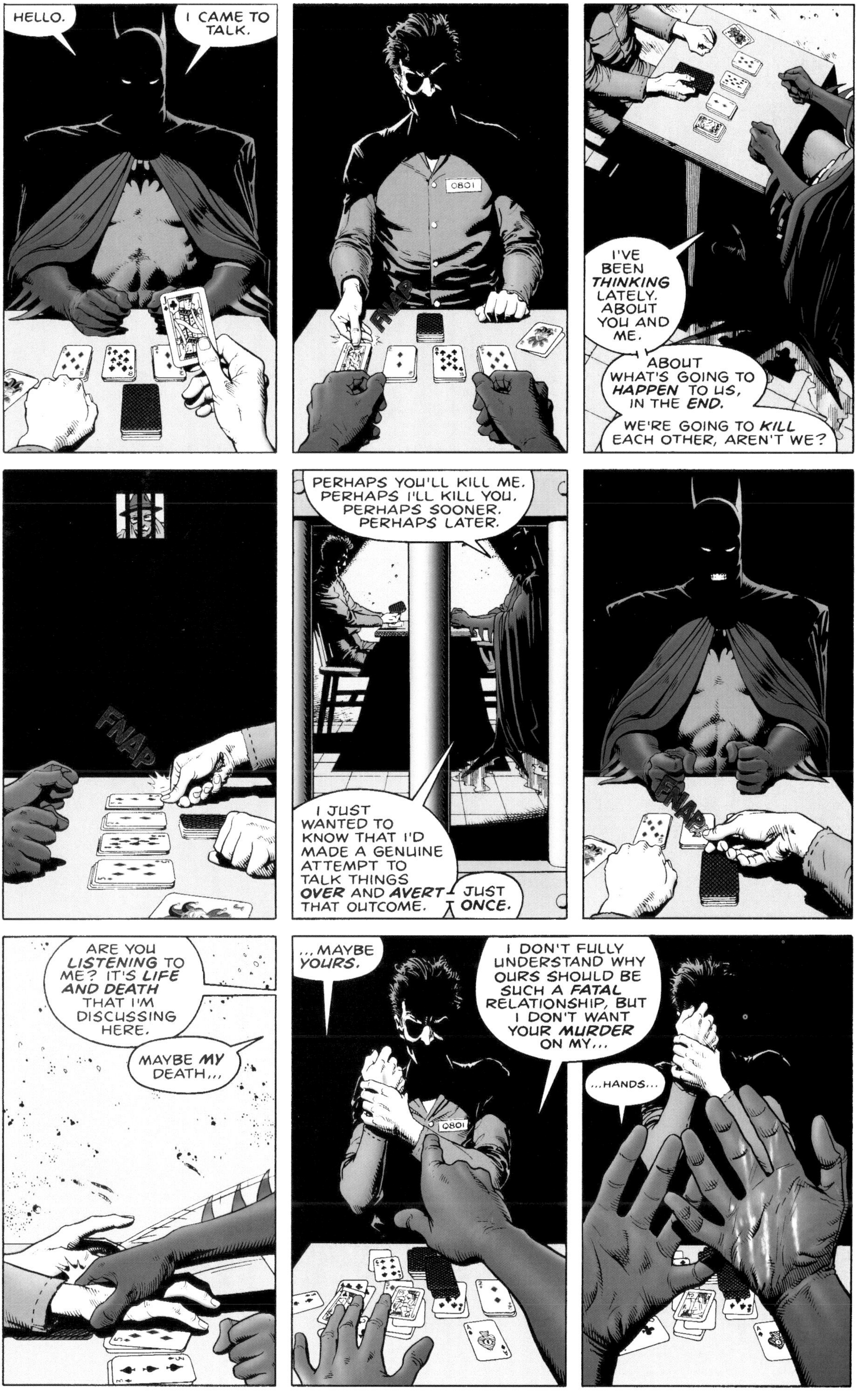
HELLO.
I CAME TO TALK.
FNAP
I'VE BEEN THINKING LATELY. ABOUT YOU AND ME.
ABOUT WHAT'S GOING TO HAPPEN TO US, IN THE END.
WE'RE GOING TO KILL EACH OTHER, AREN'T WE?
FNAP
PERHAPS YOU'LL KILL ME. PERHAPS I'LL KILL YOU. PERHAPS SOONER. PERHAPS LATER.
I JUST WANTED TO KNOW THAT I'D MADE A GENUINE ATTEMPT TO TALK THINGS OVER AND AVERT THAT OUTCOME.
JUST ONCE.
FNAP
ARE YOU LISTENING TO ME? IT'S LIFE AND DEATH THAT I'M DISCUSSING HERE.
MAYBE MY DEATH...
...MAYBE YOURS.
I DON'T FULLY UNDERSTAND WHY OURS SHOULD BE SUCH A FATAL RELATIONSHIP, BUT I DON'T WANT YOUR MURDER ON MY...
...HANDS...

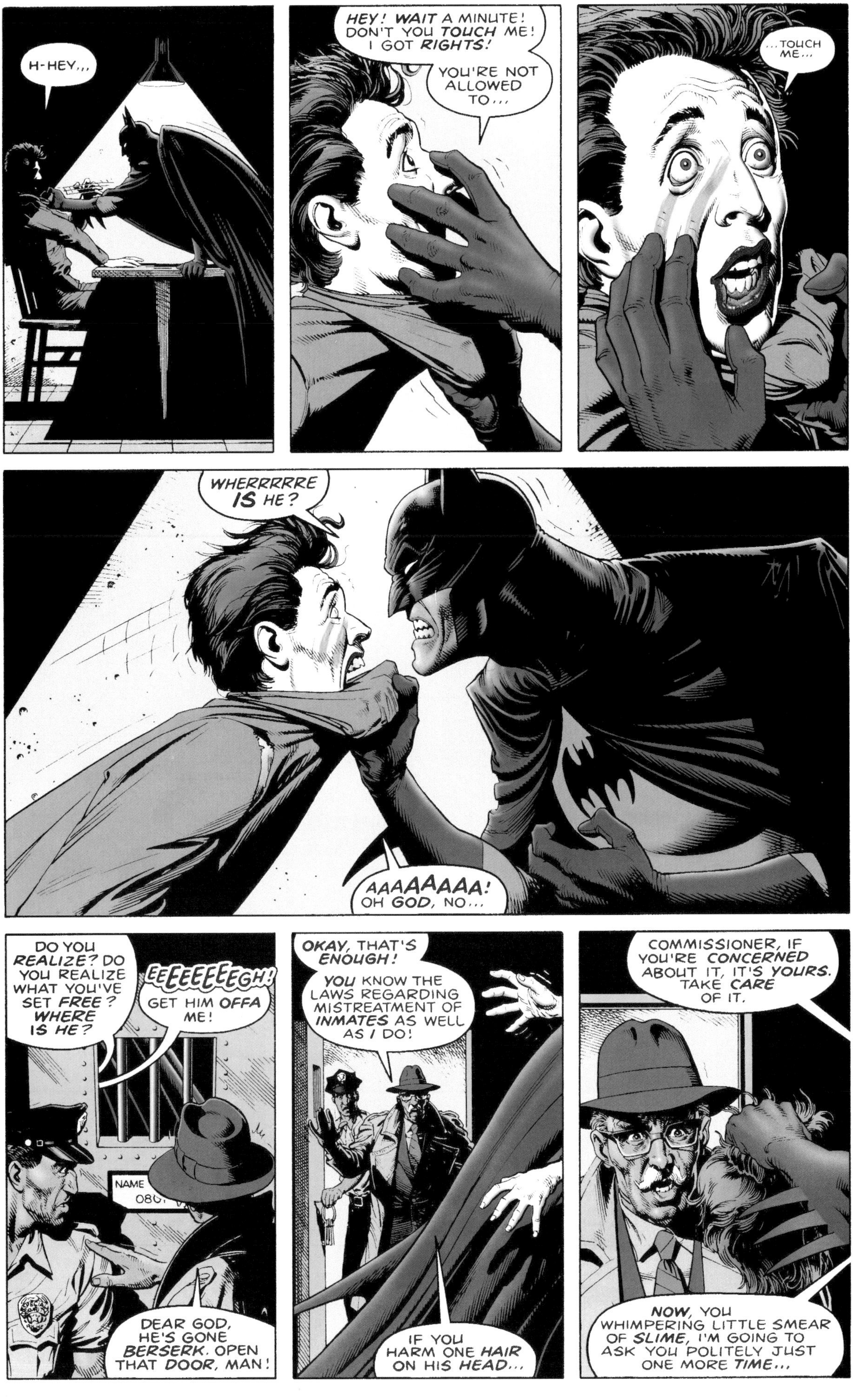
H-HEY,,,
HEY! WAIT A MINUTE! DON'T YOU TOUCH ME! I GOT RIGHTS!
YOU'RE NOT ALLOWED TO...
...TOUCH ME...
WHERRRRRE IS HE?
AAAAAAAA! OH GOD, NO...
DO YOU REALIZE? DO YOU REALIZE WHAT YOU'VE SET FREE? WHERE IS HE?
EEEEEEEGH!
GET HIM OFFA ME!
NAME
DEAR GOD, HE'S GONE BERSERK. OPEN THAT DOOR, MAN!
OKAY, THAT'S ENOUGH!
YOU KNOW THE LAWS REGARDING MISTREATMENT OF INMATES AS WELL AS I DO!
IF YOU HARM ONE HAIR ON HIS HEAD...
COMMISSIONER, IF YOU'RE CONCERNED ABOUT IT, IT'S YOURS. TAKE CARE OF IT.
NOW, YOU WHIMPERING LITTLE SMEAR OF SLIME, I'M GOING TO ASK YOU POLITELY JUST ONE MORE TIME...

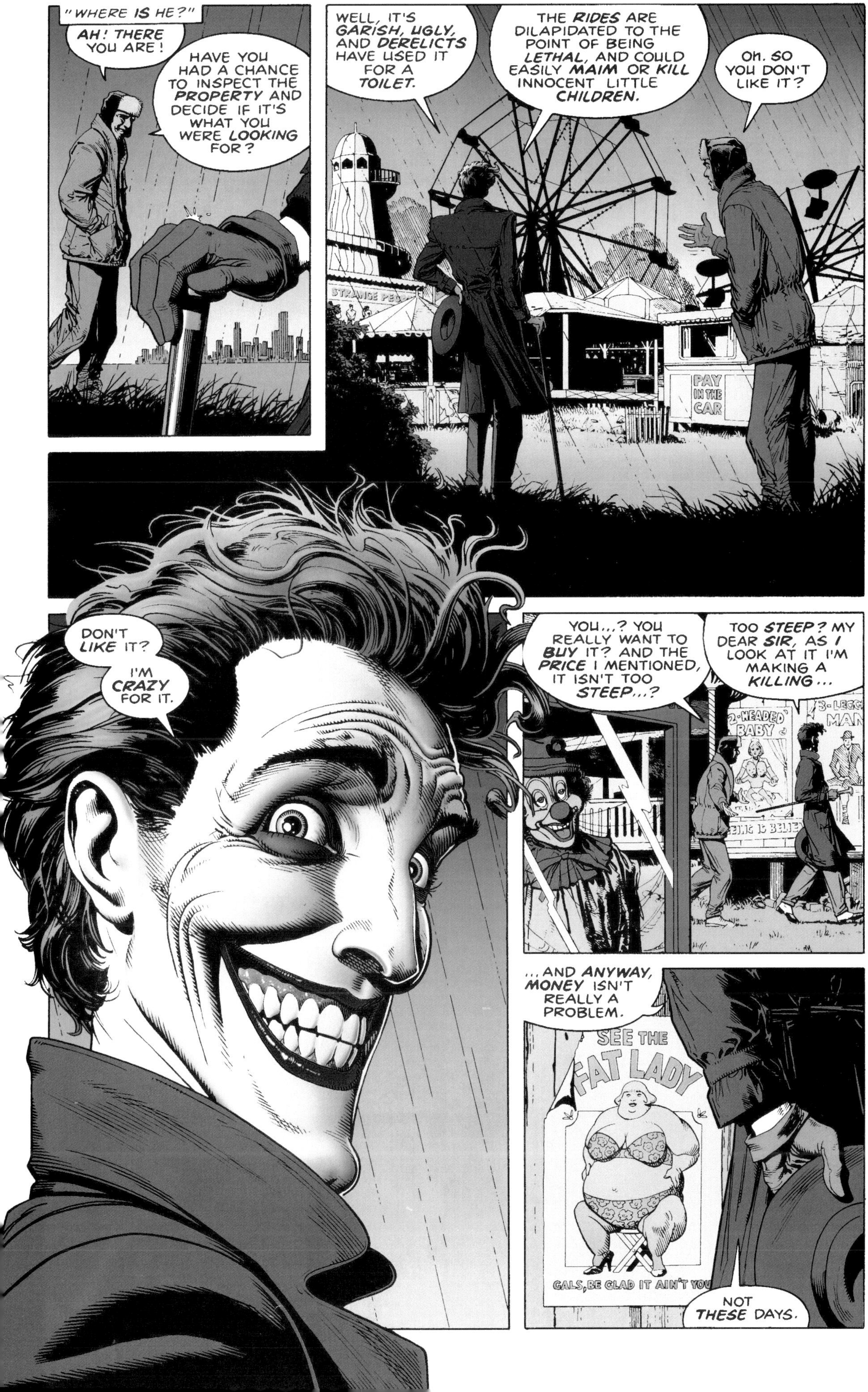
"WHERE IS HE?"
AH! THERE YOU ARE!
HAVE YOU HAD A CHANCE TO INSPECT THE PROPERTY AND DECIDE IF IT'S WHAT YOU WERE LOOKING FOR?
WELL, IT'S GARISH, UGLY, AND DERELICTS HAVE USED IT FOR A TOILET.
THE RIDES ARE DILAPIDATED TO THE POINT OF BEING LETHAL, AND COULD EASILY MAIM OR KILL INNOCENT LITTLE CHILDREN.
OH. SO YOU DON'T LIKE IT?
STRANGE PEO
PAY IN THE CAR
DON'T LIKE IT?
I'M CRAZY FOR IT.
YOU...? YOU REALLY WANT TO BUY IT? AND THE PRICE I MENTIONED, IT ISN'T TOO STEEP...?
TOO STEEP? MY DEAR SIR, AS I LOOK AT IT I'M MAKING A KILLING...
2-HEADED BABY
3-LEGG MAN
EEING IS BELIE
...AND ANYWAY, MONEY ISN'T REALLY A PROBLEM.
SEE THE FAT LADY
GALS, BE GLAD IT AIN'T YOU
NOT THESE DAYS.

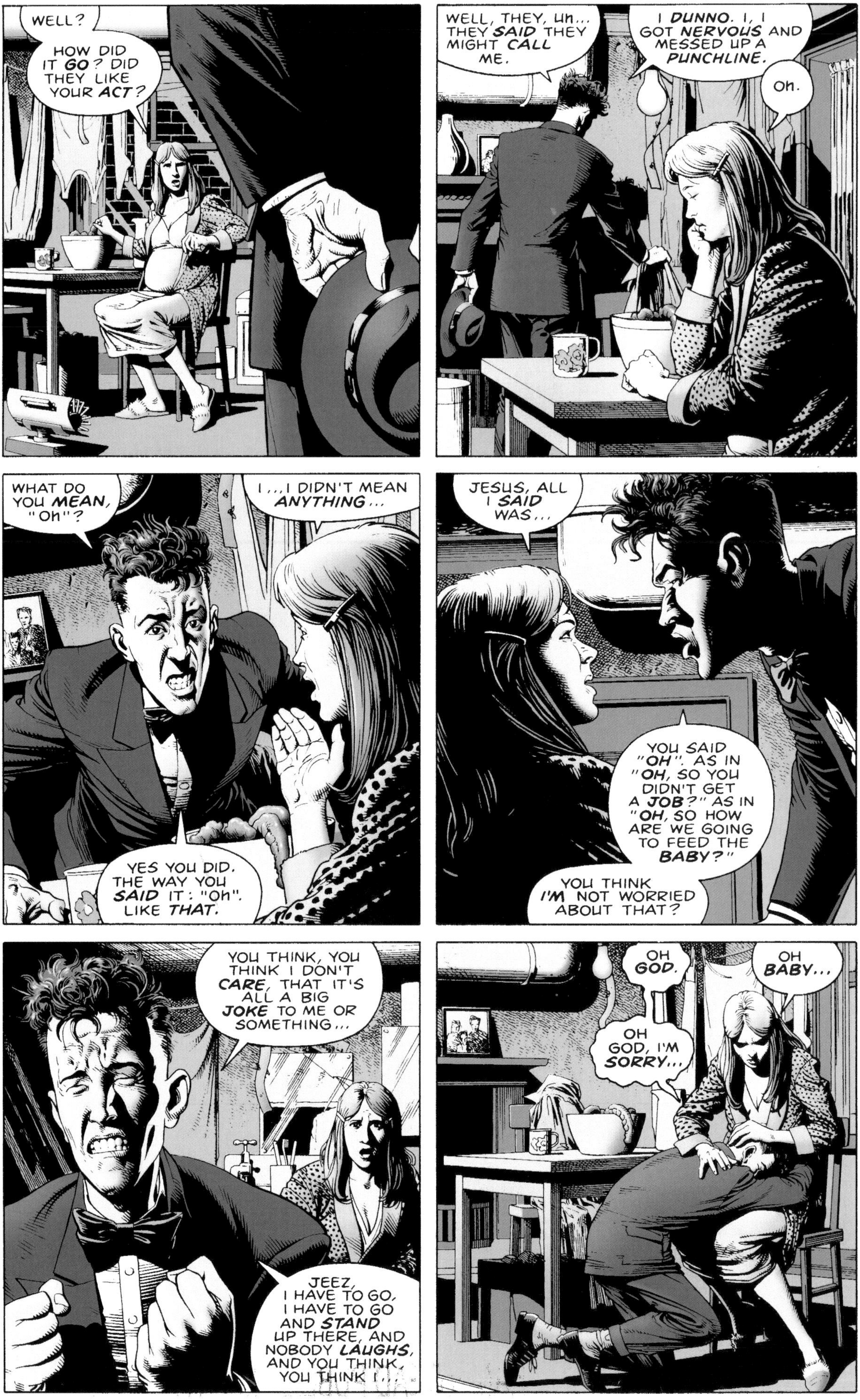
WELL?
HOW DID IT GO? DID THEY LIKE YOUR ACT?
WELL, THEY, uh... THEY SAID THEY MIGHT CALL ME.
I DUNNO. I, I GOT NERVOUS AND MESSED UP A PUNCHLINE.
Oh.
WHAT DO YOU MEAN, "Oh"?
I... I DIDN'T MEAN ANYTHING...
YES YOU DID. THE WAY YOU SAID IT: "Oh". LIKE THAT.
JESUS, ALL I SAID WAS...
YOU SAID "OH". AS IN "OH, SO YOU DIDN'T GET A JOB?" AS IN "OH, SO HOW ARE WE GOING TO FEED THE BABY?"
YOU THINK I'M NOT WORRIED ABOUT THAT?
YOU THINK, YOU THINK I DON'T CARE, THAT IT'S ALL A BIG JOKE TO ME OR SOMETHING...
JEEZ, I HAVE TO GO, I HAVE TO GO AND STAND UP THERE, AND NOBODY LAUGHS, AND YOU THINK, YOU THINK I...
OH GOD.
OH BABY...
OH GOD, I'M SORRY...

I DON'T MEAN TO TAKE IT OUT ON *YOU*. YOU'RE SUH-SUFFERING *ENOUGH*, BEING MARRIED TO A *LOSER*.

HONEY, THAT'S NOT...

IT'S *TRUE*. I CAN'T *SUPPORT* YOU. OH JEANNIE, WHAT ARE WE GOING TO *DO*?

IT'LL BE OKAY.

JUNIOR WON'T BE HERE FOR ANOTHER *THREE MONTHS*, AND I THINK *MRS. BURKISS* WILL LET THE *RENT* GO A LITTLE LONGER. SHE FEELS *SORRY* FOR ME.

SHE HATES ME.

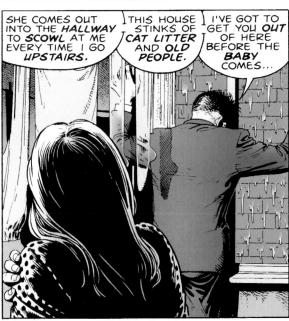

SHE COMES OUT INTO THE *HALLWAY* TO *SCOWL* AT ME EVERY TIME I GO *UPSTAIRS*.

THIS HOUSE STINKS OF *CAT LITTER* AND *OLD PEOPLE*.

I'VE GOT TO GET YOU *OUT* OF HERE BEFORE THE *BABY* COMES...

I JUST WANT ENOUGH *MONEY* TO GET SET UP IN A DECENT *NEIGHBORHOOD*.

THERE ARE GIRLS ON THE *STREET* WHO EARN THAT IN A *WEEKEND* WITHOUT HAVING TO TELL A SINGLE JOKE.

HA HA HA HA.

HONEY, DON'T *WORRY*. NOT ABOUT *ANY* OF IT. *I* STILL LOVE YOU, Y'KNOW? JOB OR *NO* JOB, YOU'RE GOOD IN THE *SACK*...

...AND YOU KNOW HOW TO MAKE ME *LAUGH*.

LAUGHING CLOWN

JUST PUT A PENNY IN THE SLOT

1

Y'KNOW, I'M *POSITIVE* YOU WON'T *REGRET* THIS PURCHASE. THE PLACE ISN'T *THAT* DILAPIDATED. SOME OF THESE *RIDES* ARE STILL PRETTY *STURDY...*

REALLY, THIS COULD BE ONE *HELL* OF A CARNIVAL.

OH, YOU'RE *SO* RIGHT.

THANKS TO YOUR SMOOTH SALESMANSHIP AND YOUR SILVER TONGUE YOU'VE COMPLETELY *SOLD* ME ON THE PLACE. LET'S *SHAKE* ON IT.

UH..., WELL, SURE. IT'S MY *PRIVILEGE...*

INDEED IT *IS.*

NATURALLY, I WON'T BE *PAYING* YOU ANYTHING. MY *COLLEAGUES* PERSUADED YOUR *PARTNER* TO SIGN THE NECESSARY *DOCUMENTS* JUST OVER AN *HOUR* AGO.

THE PROPERTY'S MINE *ALREADY.*

YOU'RE *HAPPY* WITH THAT, I TAKE IT?

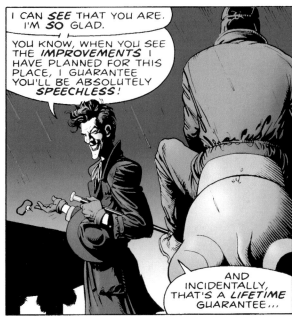

I CAN *SEE* THAT YOU ARE. I'M *SO* GLAD.

YOU KNOW, WHEN YOU SEE THE *IMPROVEMENTS* I HAVE PLANNED FOR THIS PLACE, I GUARANTEE YOU'LL BE ABSOLUTELY *SPEECHLESS!*

AND INCIDENTALLY, THAT'S A *LIFETIME* GUARANTEE...

WELL, I MUST *DASH.* THERE'S *EQUIPMENT* TO HIRE, PLUS *WORKERS* WHO'LL SUIT THE GENERAL *TONE* OF THE ESTABLISHMENT...

...AND THEN, OF COURSE, I'VE YET TO SECURE MY *MAIN ATTRACTION.*

DO FEEL FREE TO STICK *AROUND.*

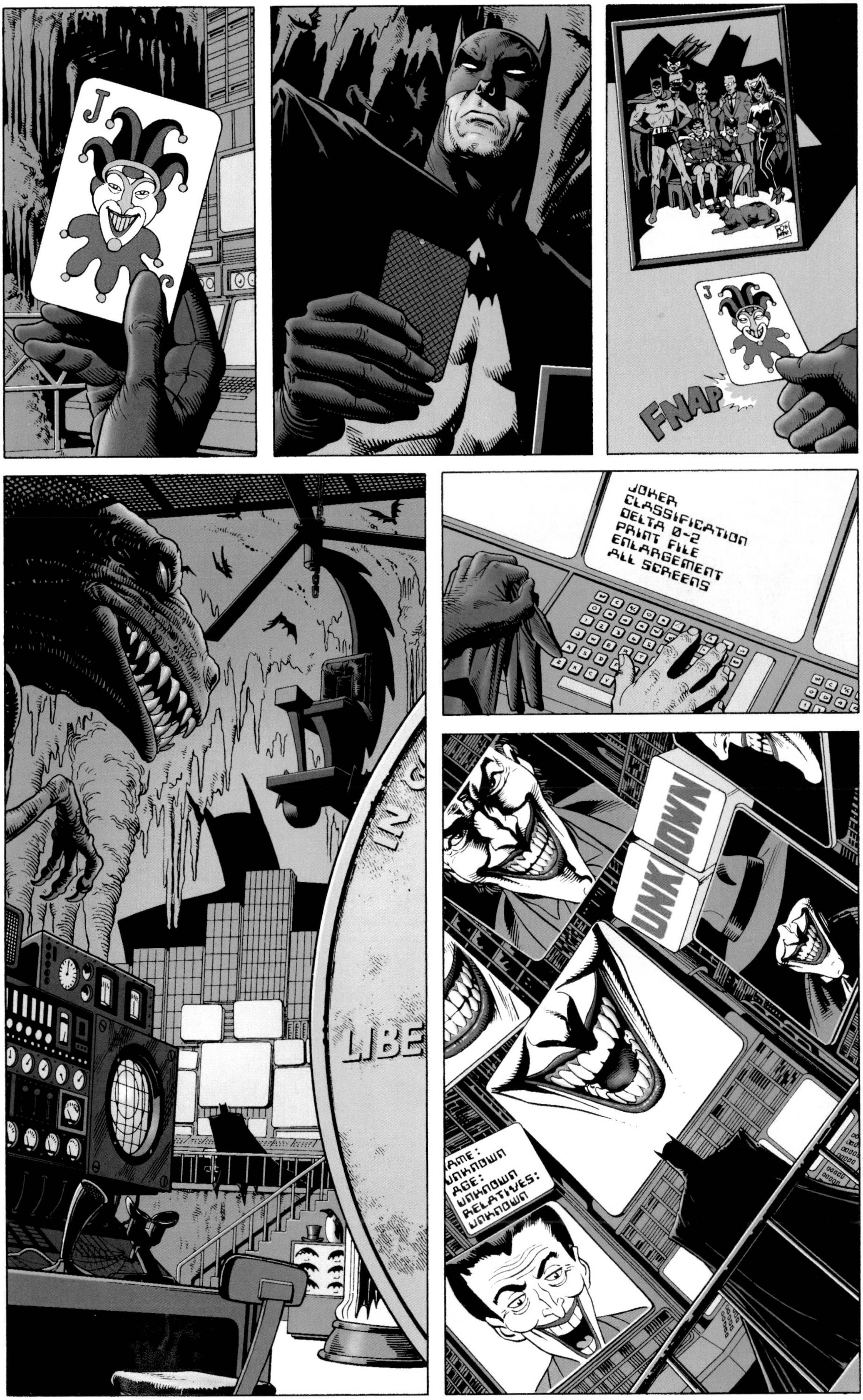
FNAP
JOKER
CLASSIFICATION
DELTA 0-2
PRINT FILE
ENLARGEMENT
ALL SCREENS
LIBE
UNKNOWN
AME:
UNKNOWN
AGE:
UNKNOWN
RELATIVES:
UNKNOWN

YOUR **REFRESHMENTS**, SIR.

MASTER **BRUCE**?

IS THERE ANYTHING **FURTHER** I CAN ASSIST WITH, OR WILL THAT BE **ALL**?

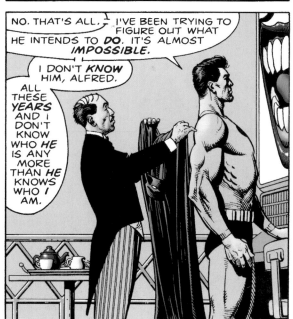

NO. THAT'S ALL. I'VE BEEN TRYING TO FIGURE OUT WHAT HE INTENDS TO **DO**. IT'S ALMOST **IMPOSSIBLE**.

I DON'T **KNOW** HIM, ALFRED.

ALL THESE **YEARS** AND I DON'T KNOW WHO **HE** IS ANY MORE THAN **HE** KNOWS WHO I AM.

HOW CAN TWO PEOPLE **HATE** SO MUCH WITHOUT **KNOWING** EACH OTHER?

I *HATE* THIS. WHENEVER WE *JAIL* HIM, I THINK "PLEASE GOD, *KEEP* HIM THERE." THEN HE *ESCAPES* AND WE ALL SIT ROUND HOPING HE WON'T DO ANYTHING *TOO* AWFUL THIS TIME.

GOTHAM EXAMINER
ASYLUM SECURITY UPROAR
MANIAC ESCAPES AGAIN
CRIMEFIGHTER UNAVAILABLE FOR COMMENT
VICKI VALE EXCLUSIVE

I *HATE* IT.

DAD, JUST *ONCE* COULD YOU LEAVE YOUR WORK AT THE *OFFICE* AND *RELAX?* I MADE YOU *COCOA*.

THANK YOU, SWEETHEART. I'LL DRINK IT WHEN I'VE PASTED THIS LATEST *CLIPPING* IN.

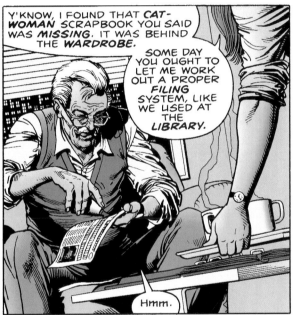

Y'KNOW, I FOUND THAT *CAT-WOMAN* SCRAPBOOK YOU SAID WAS *MISSING*. IT WAS BEHIND THE *WARDROBE*.

SOME DAY YOU OUGHT TO LET ME WORK OUT A PROPER *FILING* SYSTEM, LIKE WE USED AT THE *LIBRARY*.

Hmm.

URRGH. LOOK, YOU USED TOO MUCH *PASTE!* IT'S ALL SQUIDGING UNDER THE EDGES OF THE *CLIPPING*. YOU'RE GOING TO GET IT ON YOUR *PANTS*...

BARBARA, YOU'RE *FUSSIER* THAN YOUR *MOTHER* WA...

WAS THAT THE *DOOR?*

YEAH. IT'LL BE *COLLEEN* FROM ACROSS THE STREET. TONIGHT'S OUR *YOGA* CLASS.

C'MON, DAD,... *COMPANY!* PUT YOUR *SCRAPBOOKS* AWAY.

BAT-GARBED VIGILANTE CRITICALLY INJURES MURDERER
DISFIGURED HOMICIDAL MANIAC IN HOSPITAL

HEH. LOOK AT *THIS* ONE. FIRST TIME THEY *MET*. NOW WHAT *YEAR* WAS THAT?

WELL, I REMEMBER YOU DESCRIBING THE *WHITE* FACE AND THE *GREEN* HAIR TO ME WHEN I WAS A KID. SCARED THE *HELL* OUT OF ME.

I THOUGHT YOU'D BE *INTERESTED*...

YEAH, WELL, I HAD SOME INTERESTING *NIGHTMARES*.

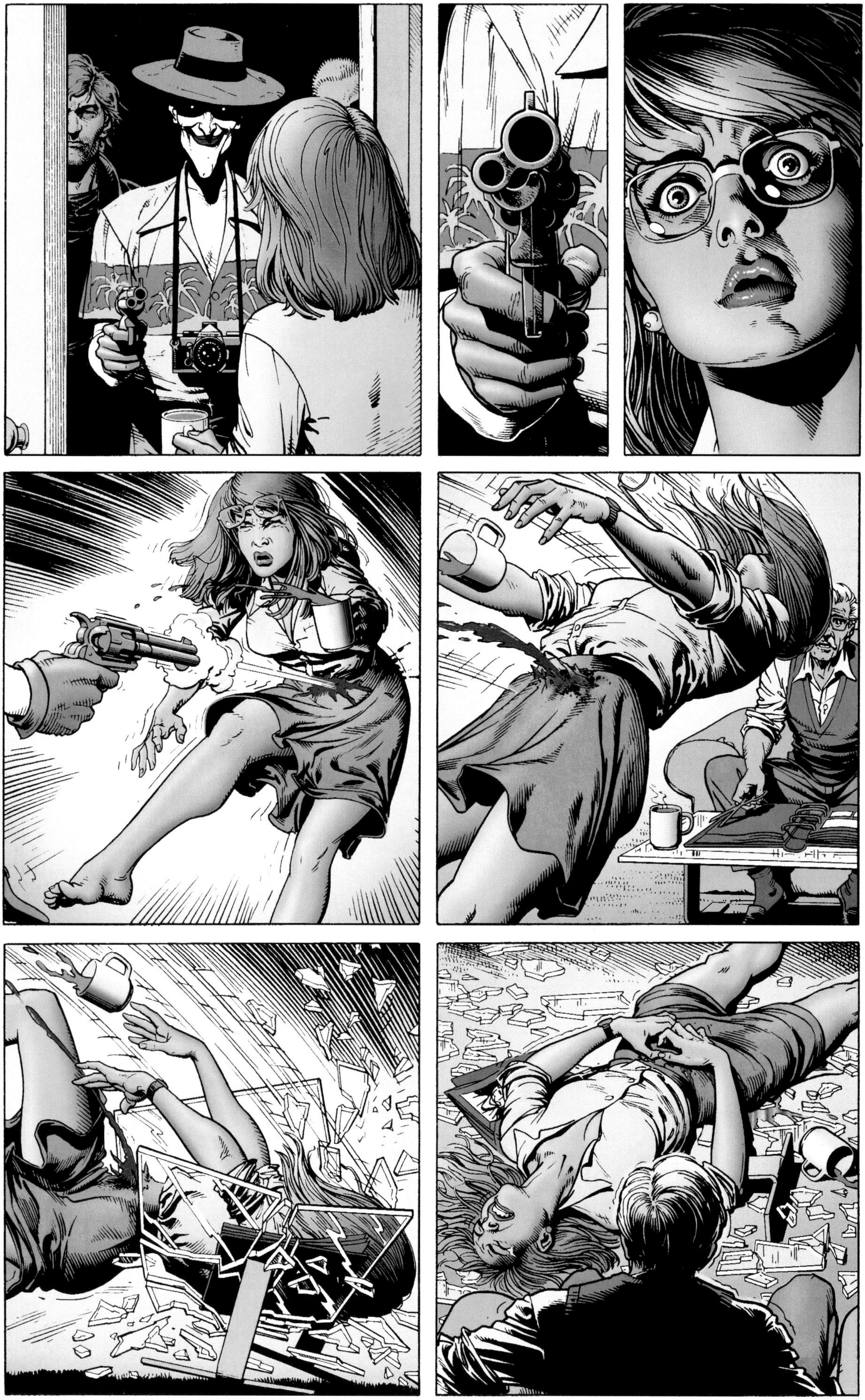

BARB..?

PLEASE DON'T *WORRY.* IT'S A *PSYCHOLOGICAL COMPLAINT,* COMMON AMONGST *EX-LIBRARIANS.* YOU SEE, SHE THINKS SHE'S A *COFFEE TABLE EDITION...*

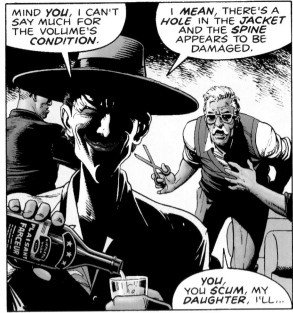

MIND *YOU,* I CAN'T SAY MUCH FOR THE VOLUME'S *CONDITION.*

I *MEAN,* THERE'S A *HOLE* IN THE *JACKET* AND THE *SPINE* APPEARS TO BE *DAMAGED.*

YOU, YOU *SCUM,* MY *DAUGHTER,* I'LL...

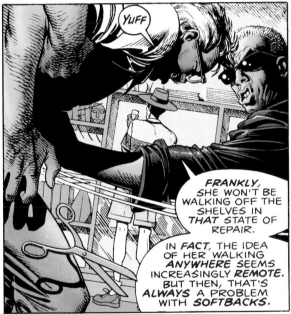

YUFF

FRANKLY, SHE WON'T BE WALKING OFF THE SHELVES IN *THAT* STATE OF *REPAIR.*

IN *FACT,* THE IDEA OF HER WALKING *ANYWHERE* SEEMS INCREASINGLY *REMOTE.* BUT THEN, THAT'S *ALWAYS* A PROBLEM WITH *SOFTBACKS.*

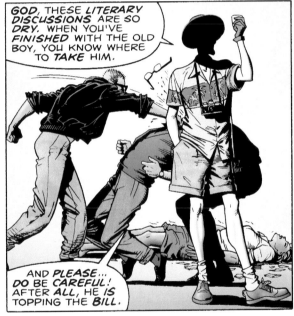

GOD, THESE *LITERARY DISCUSSIONS* ARE SO *DRY.* WHEN YOU'VE *FINISHED* WITH THE OLD BOY, YOU KNOW WHERE TO *TAKE* HIM.

AND *PLEASE...* DO BE CAREFUL! AFTER ALL, HE *IS* TOPPING THE *BILL.*

YOU KNOW, IT'S *SUCH* A SHAME YOU'LL MISS YOUR FATHER'S *DEBUT,* MISS GORDON.

SADLY, OUR *VENUE* WASN'T *BUILT* WITH THE *DISABLED* IN MIND.

BUT DON'T *WORRY...* I'LL TAKE SOME *SNAPSHOTS* TO *REMIND* HIM OF *YOU.*

WUH... WUH...WHY... ARE YOU...

DUH... *DOING* THIS..?

TO PROVE A *POINT.*

HERE'S TO *CRIME.*

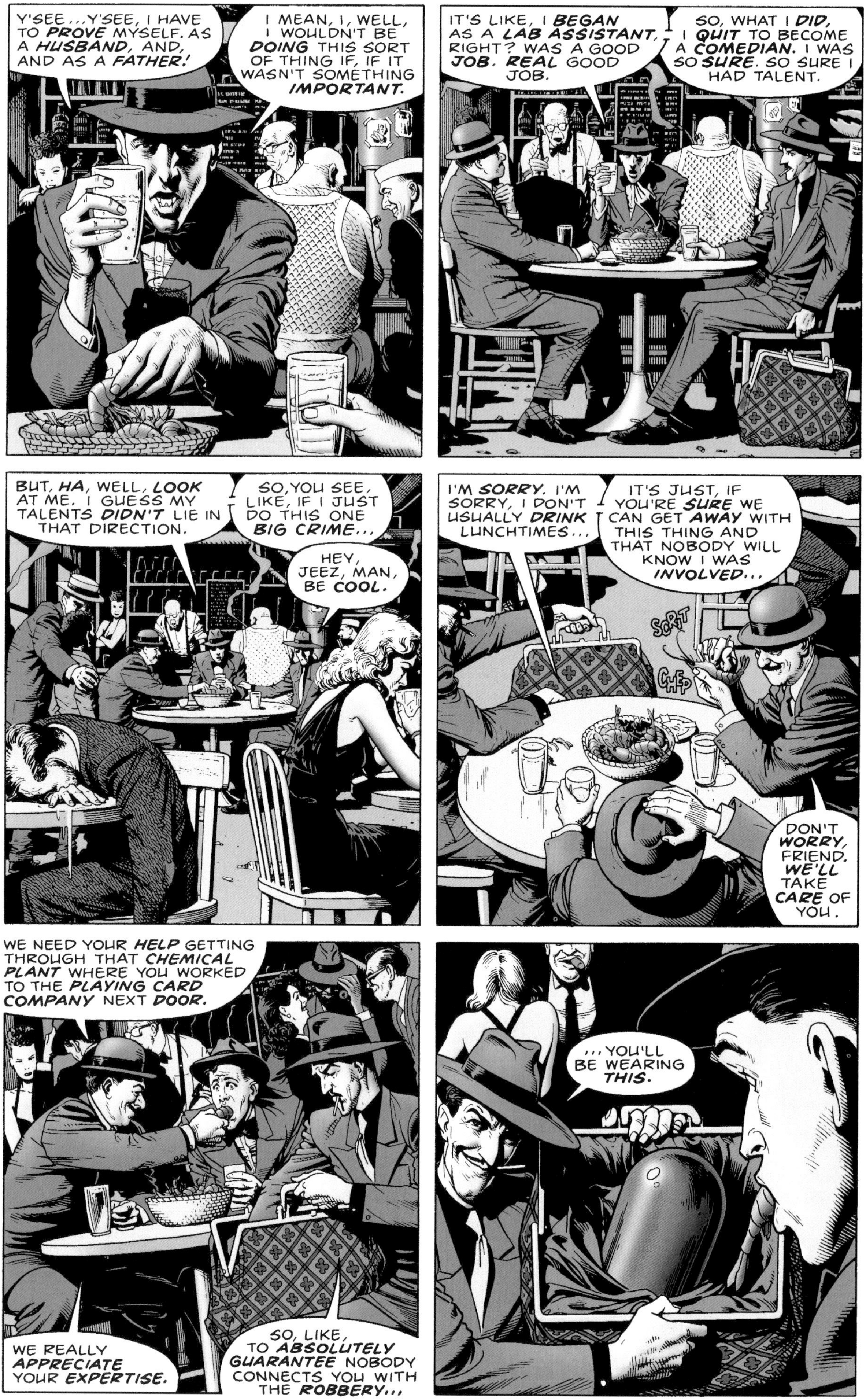

Y'SEE... Y'SEE, I HAVE TO PROVE MYSELF. AS A HUSBAND, AND, AND AS A FATHER!
I MEAN, I, WELL, I WOULDN'T BE DOING THIS SORT OF THING IF, IF IT WASN'T SOMETHING IMPORTANT.
IT'S LIKE, I BEGAN AS A LAB ASSISTANT, RIGHT? WAS A GOOD JOB. REAL GOOD JOB.
SO, WHAT I DID, I QUIT TO BECOME A COMEDIAN. I WAS SO SURE. SO SURE I HAD TALENT.
BUT, HA, WELL, LOOK AT ME. I GUESS MY TALENTS DIDN'T LIE IN THAT DIRECTION.
SO, YOU SEE, LIKE, IF I JUST DO THIS ONE BIG CRIME...
HEY, JEEZ, MAN, BE COOL.
I'M SORRY. I'M SORRY, I DON'T USUALLY DRINK LUNCHTIMES...
IT'S JUST, IF YOU'RE SURE WE CAN GET AWAY WITH THIS THING AND THAT NOBODY WILL KNOW I WAS INVOLVED...
SCRT
CHEP
DON'T WORRY, FRIEND. WE'LL TAKE CARE OF YOU.
WE NEED YOUR HELP GETTING THROUGH THAT CHEMICAL PLANT WHERE YOU WORKED TO THE PLAYING CARD COMPANY NEXT DOOR.
WE REALLY APPRECIATE YOUR EXPERTISE.
SO, LIKE, TO ABSOLUTELY GUARANTEE NOBODY CONNECTS YOU WITH THE ROBBERY...
...YOU'LL BE WEARING THIS.

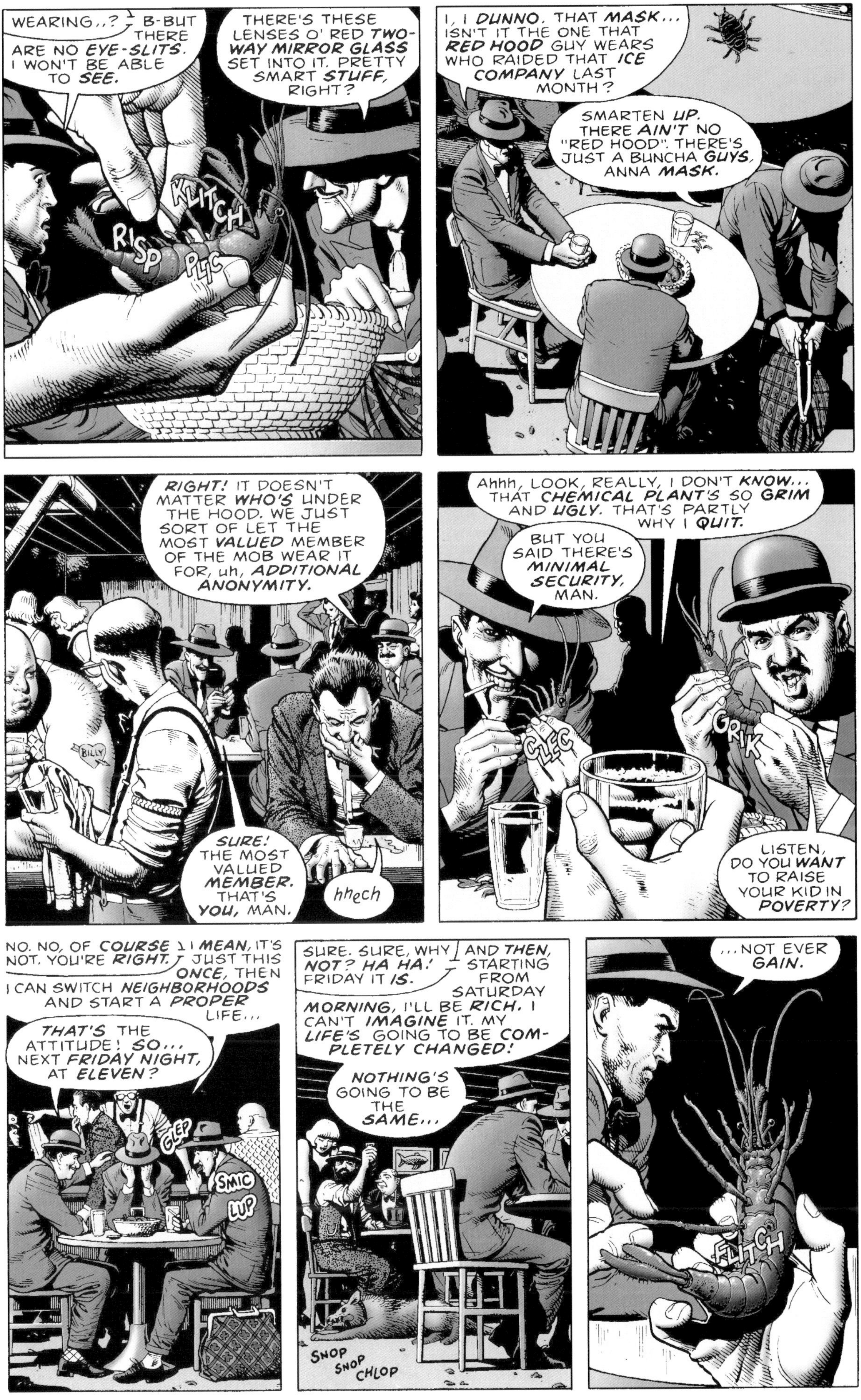
WEARING..? B-BUT THERE ARE NO EYE-SLITS. I WON'T BE ABLE TO SEE.
THERE'S THESE LENSES O' RED TWO-WAY MIRROR GLASS SET INTO IT. PRETTY SMART STUFF, RIGHT?
KLITCH
RISP
PLIC
I, I DUNNO. THAT MASK... ISN'T IT THE ONE THAT RED HOOD GUY WEARS WHO RAIDED THAT ICE COMPANY LAST MONTH?
SMARTEN UP. THERE AIN'T NO "RED HOOD". THERE'S JUST A BUNCHA GUYS, ANNA MASK.
RIGHT! IT DOESN'T MATTER WHO'S UNDER THE HOOD. WE JUST SORT OF LET THE MOST VALUED MEMBER OF THE MOB WEAR IT FOR, uh, ADDITIONAL ANONYMITY.
BILLY
SURE! THE MOST VALUED MEMBER. THAT'S YOU, MAN.
hhech
Ahhh, LOOK, REALLY, I DON'T KNOW... THAT CHEMICAL PLANT'S SO GRIM AND UGLY. THAT'S PARTLY WHY I QUIT.
BUT YOU SAID THERE'S MINIMAL SECURITY, MAN.
CLIC
GRIK
LISTEN, DO YOU WANT TO RAISE YOUR KID IN POVERTY?
NO. NO, OF COURSE NOT. YOU'RE RIGHT.
I MEAN, IT'S JUST THIS ONCE, THEN I CAN SWITCH NEIGHBORHOODS AND START A PROPER LIFE...
THAT'S THE ATTITUDE! SO... NEXT FRIDAY NIGHT, AT ELEVEN?
GLEP
SMIC
LUP
SURE. SURE, WHY NOT? HA HA! FRIDAY IT IS.
AND THEN, STARTING FROM SATURDAY MORNING, I'LL BE RICH. I CAN'T IMAGINE IT. MY LIFE'S GOING TO BE COMPLETELY CHANGED!
NOTHING'S GOING TO BE THE SAME...
SNOP
SNOP
CHLOP
...NOT EVER GAIN.
FLITCH

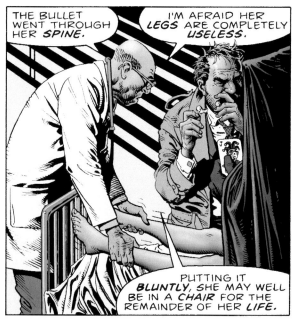

THE BULLET WENT THROUGH HER *SPINE*.

I'M AFRAID HER *LEGS* ARE COMPLETELY *USELESS*.

PUTTING IT *BLUNTLY*, SHE MAY WELL BE IN A *CHAIR* FOR THE REMAINDER OF HER *LIFE*.

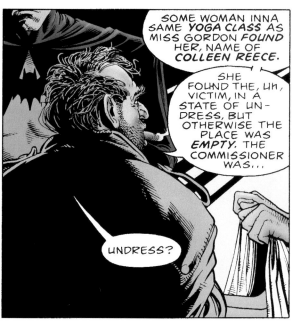

SOME WOMAN INNA SAME *YOGA CLASS* AS MISS GORDON *FOUND* HER, NAME OF *COLLEEN REECE*.

SHE FOUND THE, UH, VICTIM, IN A STATE OF UN-DRESS, BUT OTHERWISE THE PLACE WAS *EMPTY*. THE COMMISSIONER WAS...

UNDRESS?

THEY DIDN'T *TELL* YOU? HE'D REMOVED HER *CLOTHING* AFTER *SHOOTING* HER. WE, UH,... WELL, WE FOUND A *LENS-CAP* ON THE FLOOR THAT DIDN'T FIT ANY CAMERA IN THE PLACE. WE BELIEVE THAT, UHH,...

WELL, THAT HE TOOK SOME *PICTURES*.

OF HER.

JEEZ, LOOK, REALLY, I'M *SORRY*. I THOUGHT YOU *KNEW*. IT'S PRETTY *SICK*, AIN'T IT?

YES.

PRETTY SICK.

PLEASE LEAVE US ALONE FOR A MOMENT.

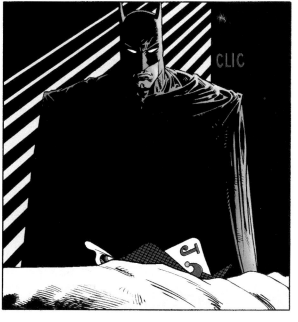

CLIC

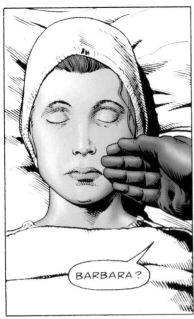

BARBARA?

BARBARA, CAN YOU *HEAR* ME?

IT'S ME.

IT'S *BRUCE*.

BRUCE..?

BRUCE.... IT WAS *HIM* ... TOOK *DAD* ...H-HE...

Oh *GOD!* Oh GOD, I *REMEMBER!* Oh, *BRUCE,* WHAT HE *DID*...

BARBARA, TAKE IT *EASY.* IT'S *OKAY*...

NO! NO, IT'S *NOT* OKAY! HE'S... HE'S TAKING IT TO THE *LIMIT* THIS TIME...

YOU DIDN'T *SEE.*

YOU DIDN'T SEE HIS *EYES.*

H-HE SAID HE WANTED TO PUH-*PROVE* A *POINT*... SAID ...DAD WAS... TOP OF THE *BILL*...

WH-WHAT'S HE *DOING* TO HIM, BRUCE?

WHAT'S HE DOING TO MY *FATHER?*

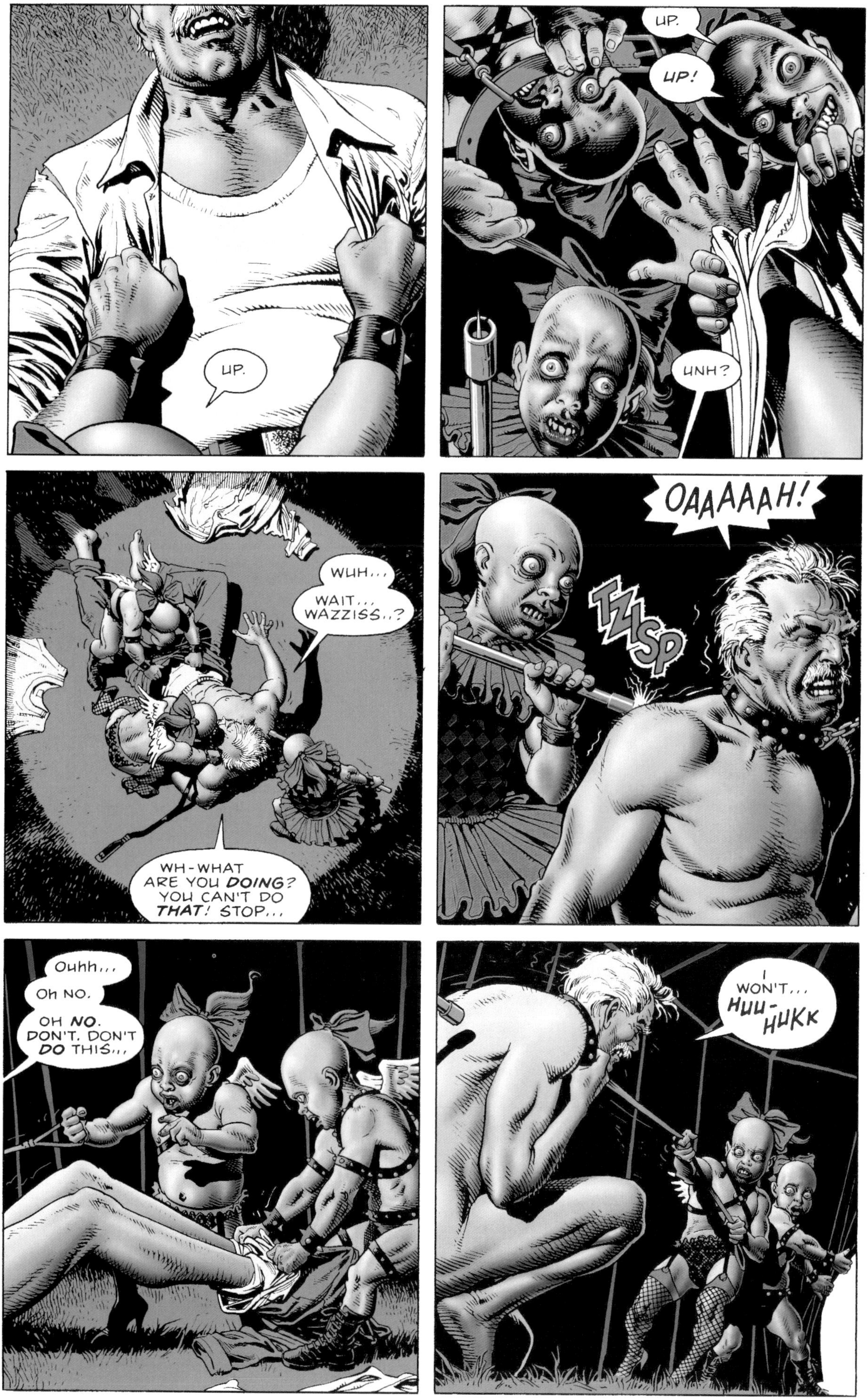
UP.
UP.
UP!
UNH?
WUH... WAIT... WAZZISS..?
WH-WHAT ARE YOU DOING? YOU CAN'T DO THAT! STOP...
OAAAAAH!
TZZSP
Ouhh...
Oh NO.
OH NO. DON'T. DON'T DO THIS...
I WON'T... HUU-HUKK

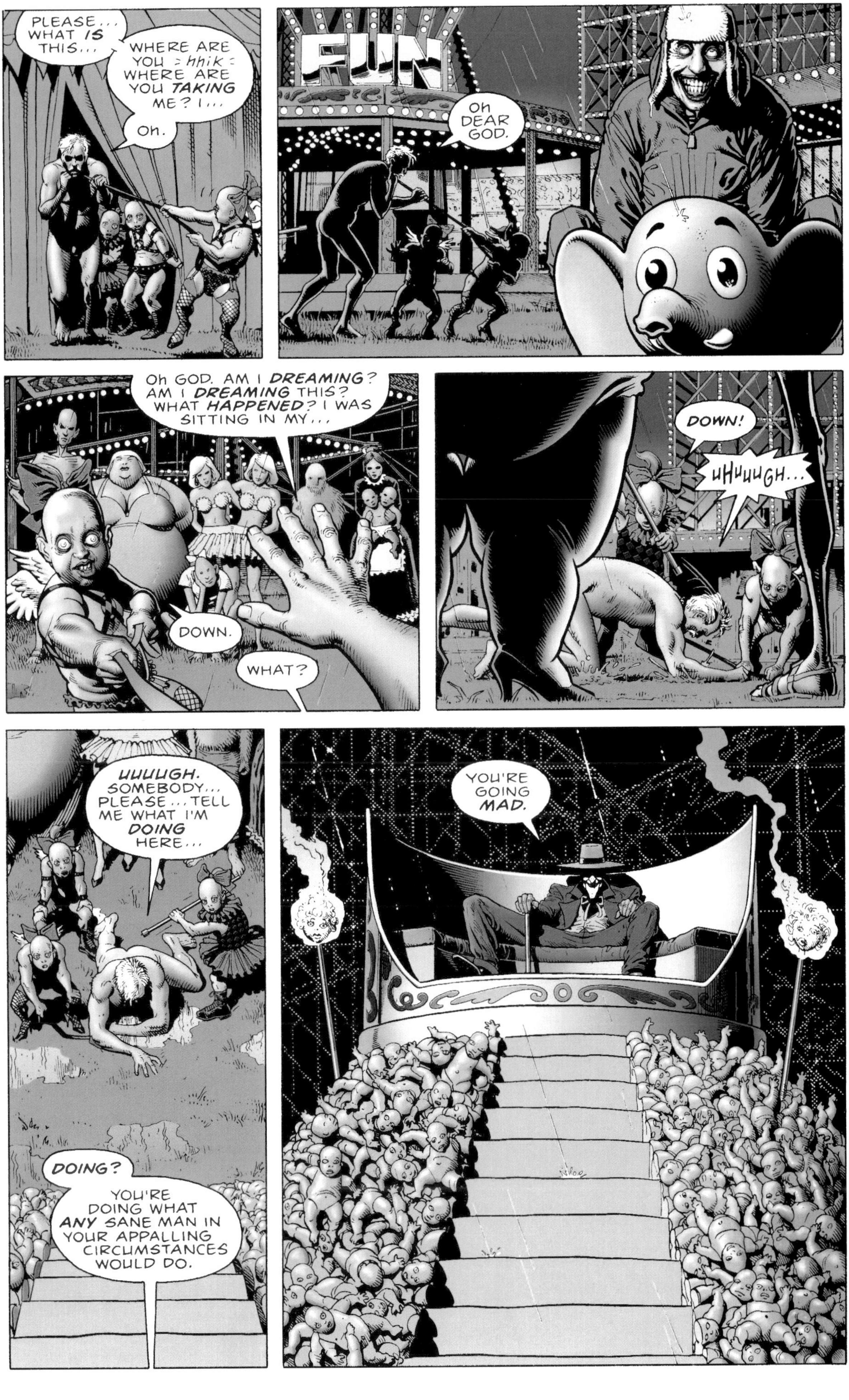

PLEASE... WHAT *IS* THIS...
WHERE ARE YOU :hhik: WHERE ARE YOU *TAKING* ME? I...
Oh.
FUN
Oh DEAR GOD.
Oh GOD. AM I *DREAMING*? AM I *DREAMING* THIS? WHAT *HAPPENED*? I WAS SITTING IN MY...
DOWN.
WHAT?
DOWN!
UHUUUGH...
UUUUGH. SOMEBODY... PLEASE... TELL ME WHAT I'M *DOING* HERE...
DOING?
YOU'RE DOING WHAT *ANY* SANE MAN IN YOUR APPALLING CIRCUMSTANCES WOULD DO.
YOU'RE GOING *MAD.*

YOU.

Oh no. I... I REMEMBER.

REMEMBER? OHH, I WOULDN'T DO THAT! REMEMBERING'S DANGEROUS. I FIND THE PAST SUCH A WORRYING, ANXIOUS PLACE.

"THE PAST TENSE," I SUPPOSE YOU'D CALL IT. HA HA HA.

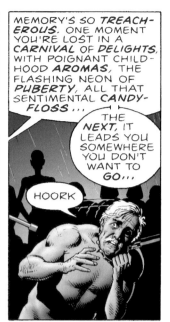

MEMORY'S SO TREACHEROUS. ONE MOMENT YOU'RE LOST IN A CARNIVAL OF DELIGHTS, WITH POIGNANT CHILDHOOD AROMAS, THE FLASHING NEON OF PUBERTY, ALL THAT SENTIMENTAL CANDY-FLOSS...

THE NEXT, IT LEADS YOU SOMEWHERE YOU DON'T WANT TO GO...

HOORK

...SOMEWHERE DARK AND COLD, FILLED WITH THE DAMP, AMBIGUOUS SHAPES OF THINGS YOU'D HOPED WERE FORGOTTEN.

GHOST TRA

MEMORIES CAN BE VILE, REPULSIVE LITTLE BRUTES. LIKE CHILDREN, I SUPPOSE. HAHA.

BARBARA. Oh NO. Oh NO...

BUT CAN WE LIVE WITHOUT THEM? MEMORIES ARE WHAT OUR REASON IS BASED UPON. IF WE CAN'T FACE THEM, WE DENY REASON ITSELF!

ALTHOUGH, WHY NOT? WE AREN'T CONTRACTUALLY TIED DOWN TO RATIONALITY!

THERE IS NO SANITY CLAUSE!

SO WHEN YOU FIND YOURSELF LOCKED ONTO AN UNPLEASANT TRAIN OF THOUGHT, HEADING FOR THE PLACES IN YOUR PAST WHERE THE SCREAMING IS UNBEARABLE, REMEMBER THERE'S ALWAYS MADNESS.

MADNESS IS THE EMERGENCY EXIT...

YOU CAN JUST STEP OUTSIDE, AND CLOSE THE DOOR ON ALL THOSE DREADFUL THINGS THAT HAPPENED. YOU CAN LOCK THEM AWAY...

FOREVER.

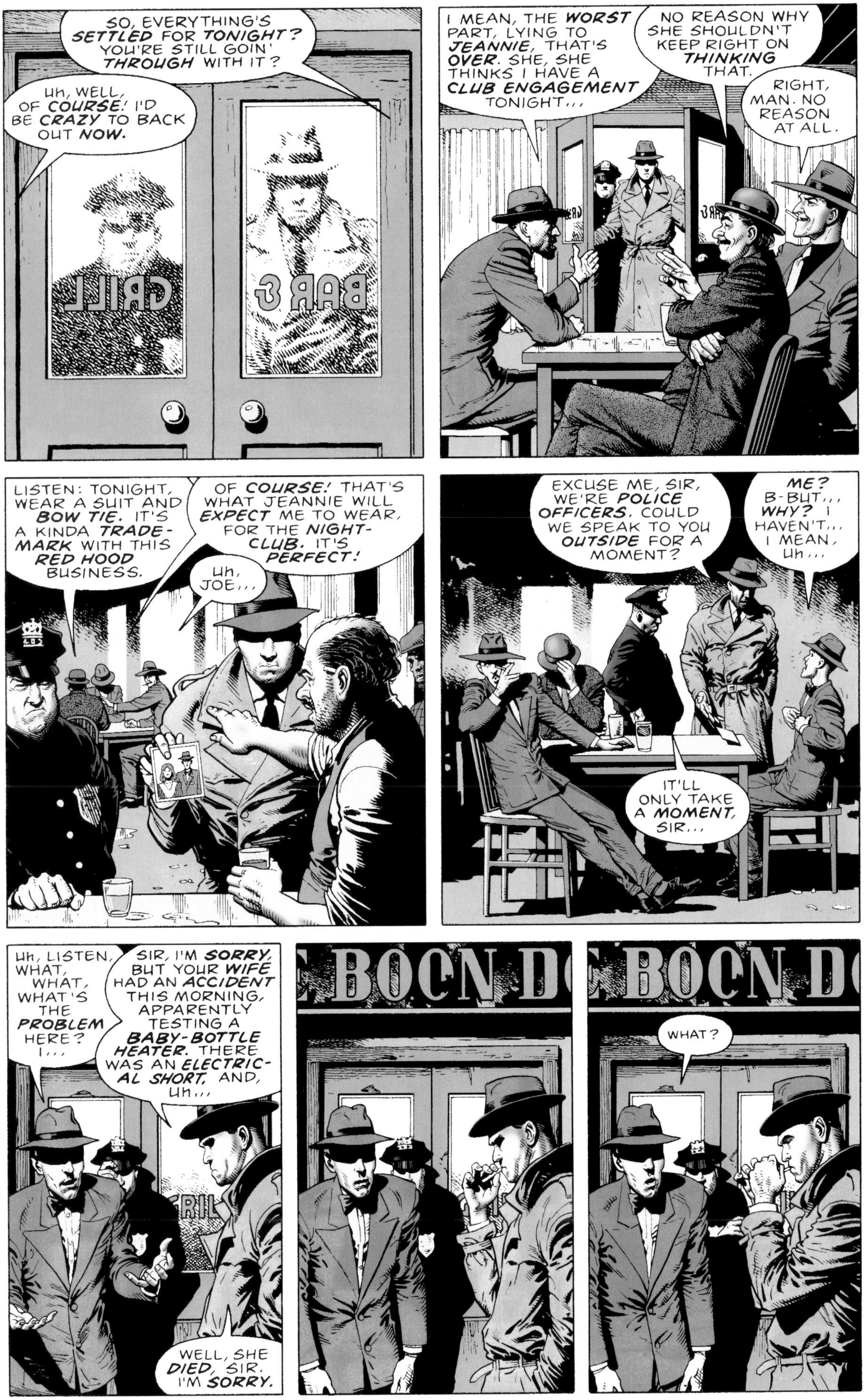
SO, EVERYTHING'S SETTLED FOR TONIGHT? YOU'RE STILL GOIN' THROUGH WITH IT?
UH, WELL, OF COURSE! I'D BE CRAZY TO BACK OUT NOW.
GRILL
BAR &
I MEAN, THE WORST PART, LYING TO JEANNIE, THAT'S OVER. SHE, SHE THINKS I HAVE A CLUB ENGAGEMENT TONIGHT...
NO REASON WHY SHE SHOULDN'T KEEP RIGHT ON THINKING THAT.
RIGHT, MAN. NO REASON AT ALL.
LISTEN: TONIGHT, WEAR A SUIT AND BOW TIE. IT'S A KINDA TRADE-MARK WITH THIS RED HOOD BUSINESS.
OF COURSE! THAT'S WHAT JEANNIE WILL EXPECT ME TO WEAR, FOR THE NIGHT-CLUB. IT'S PERFECT!
UH, JOE...
EXCUSE ME, SIR, WE'RE POLICE OFFICERS. COULD WE SPEAK TO YOU OUTSIDE FOR A MOMENT?
ME? B-BUT... WHY? I HAVEN'T... I MEAN, UH...
IT'LL ONLY TAKE A MOMENT, SIR...
UH, LISTEN, WHAT, WHAT, WHAT'S THE PROBLEM HERE? I...
SIR, I'M SORRY. BUT YOUR WIFE HAD AN ACCIDENT THIS MORNING, APPARENTLY TESTING A BABY-BOTTLE HEATER. THERE WAS AN ELECTRIC-AL SHORT, AND, UH...
WELL, SHE DIED, SIR. I'M SORRY.
E BOCN DC
C BOCN DC
WHAT?

LISTEN, I *HATE* TO *BREAK* IT TO YOU LIKE THIS. IT WAS A *MILLION TO ONE ACCIDENT!* THEY HAVE *FULL DETAILS* WAITING FOR YOU AT THE *HOSPITAL.*

THERE'S NO *HURRY.*

IF *I* WAS YOU, I'D HAVE ANOTHER *DRINK.*

MY WIFE.

SHE'S *DEAD.* MY WIFE...

GEE, THAT'S *TERRIBLE.* WE'RE REALLY *SORRY.*

YEAH. HEY, LISTEN, MAN, YOU PROBABLY WANNA BE LEFT *ALONE* RIGHT NOW, HUH? WE'LL SEE YOU HERE *TONIGHT,* OKAY?

TONIGHT? BUT... BUT I CAN'T DO ANYTHING *TONIGHT.* TH-THERE'S NO *REASON* ANYMORE. JEANNIE... JEANNIE... JEANNIE'S *DEAD.* YOU DON'T *UNDERSTAND...*

NO, NO, NO. NO, I'M *SORRY* ABOUT YOUR *WIFE,* BUT IT'S *YOU* THAT DON'T *UNDERSTAND.*

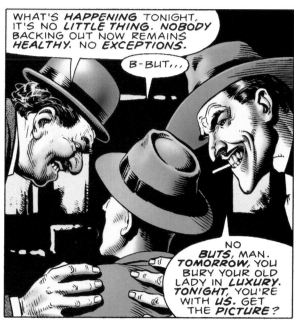

WHAT'S *HAPPENING* TONIGHT, IT'S NO *LITTLE THING.* NOBODY BACKING OUT NOW REMAINS *HEALTHY.* NO *EXCEPTIONS.*

B-BUT...

NO *BUTS,* MAN. *TOMORROW,* YOU BURY YOUR OLD LADY IN *LUXURY.* TONIGHT, YOU'RE WITH *US.* GET THE *PICTURE?*

YES.

YES, I GET THE PICTURE.

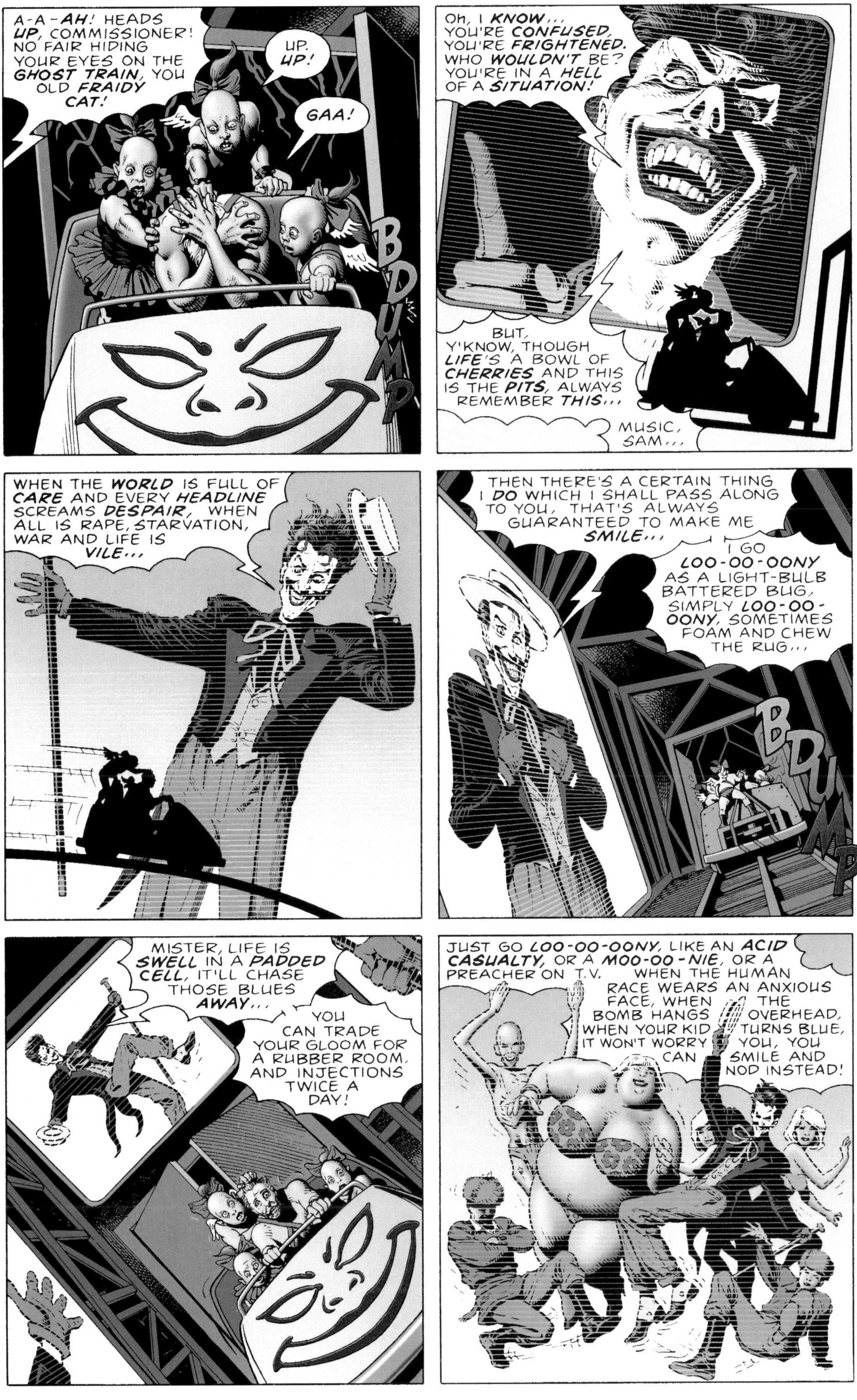

A-A-AH! HEADS UP, COMMISSIONER! NO FAIR HIDING YOUR EYES ON THE GHOST TRAIN, YOU OLD FRAIDY CAT!
UP. UP!
GAA!
BDUMP
Oh, I KNOW... YOU'RE CONFUSED, YOU'RE FRIGHTENED. WHO WOULDN'T BE? YOU'RE IN A HELL OF A SITUATION!
BUT, Y'KNOW, THOUGH LIFE'S A BOWL OF CHERRIES AND THIS IS THE PITS, ALWAYS REMEMBER THIS...
MUSIC, SAM...
WHEN THE WORLD IS FULL OF CARE AND EVERY HEADLINE SCREAMS DESPAIR, WHEN ALL IS RAPE, STARVATION, WAR AND LIFE IS VILE...
THEN THERE'S A CERTAIN THING I DO WHICH I SHALL PASS ALONG TO YOU, THAT'S ALWAYS GUARANTEED TO MAKE ME SMILE...
I GO LOO-OO-OONY AS A LIGHT-BULB BATTERED BUG, SIMPLY LOO-OO-OONY, SOMETIMES FOAM AND CHEW THE RUG...
BDUMP
MISTER, LIFE IS SWELL IN A PADDED CELL, IT'LL CHASE THOSE BLUES AWAY...
YOU CAN TRADE YOUR GLOOM FOR A RUBBER ROOM, AND INJECTIONS TWICE A DAY!
JUST GO LOO-OO-OONY, LIKE AN ACID CASUALTY, OR A MOO-OO-NIE, OR A PREACHER ON T.V.
WHEN THE HUMAN RACE WEARS AN ANXIOUS FACE, WHEN THE BOMB HANGS OVERHEAD, WHEN YOUR KID TURNS BLUE, IT WON'T WORRY YOU, YOU CAN SMILE AND NOD INSTEAD!

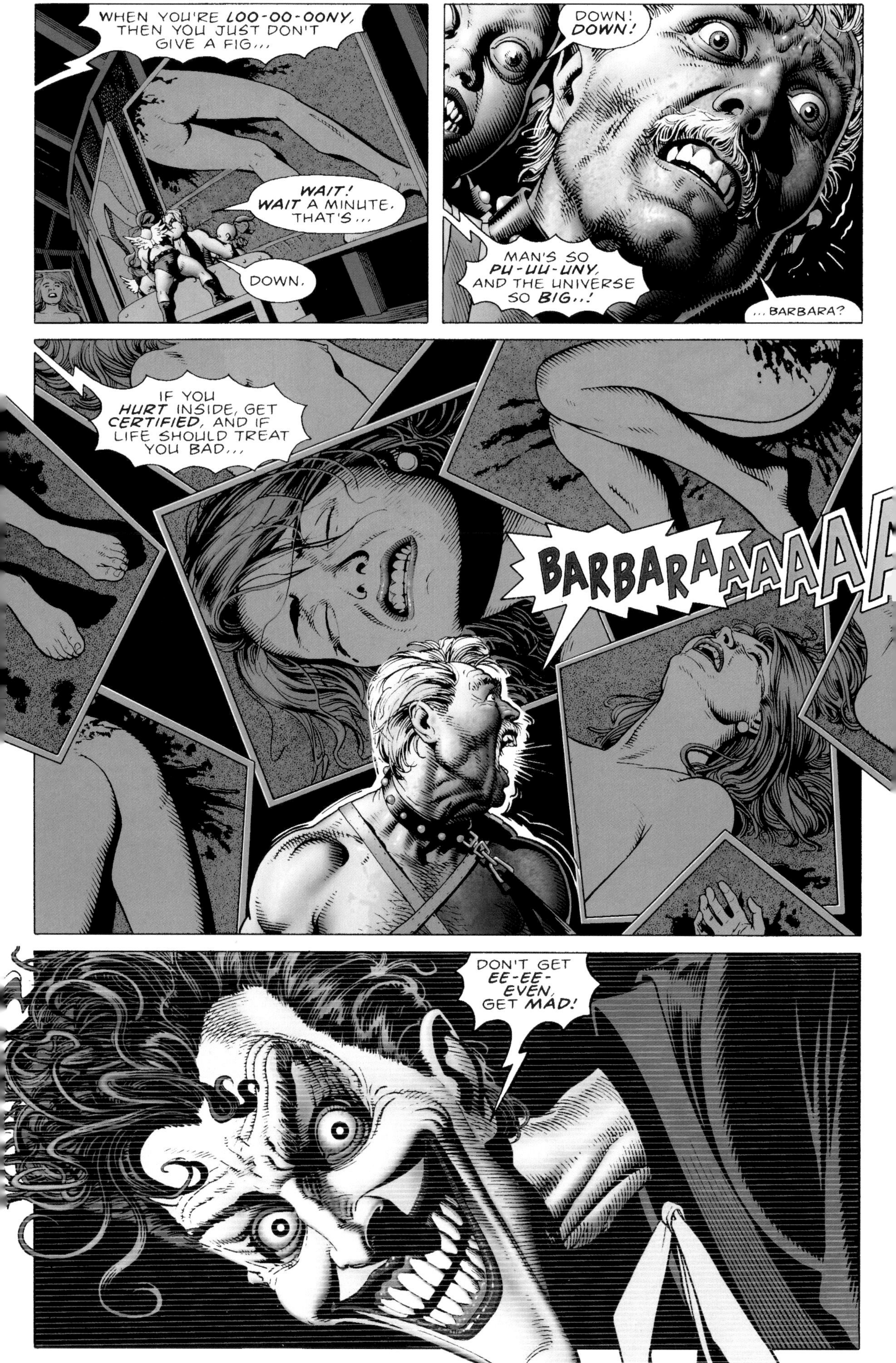
WHEN YOU'RE LOO-OO-OONY, THEN YOU JUST DON'T GIVE A FIG...
WAIT! WAIT A MINUTE. THAT'S...
DOWN.
DOWN! DOWN!
MAN'S SO PU-UU-UNY, AND THE UNIVERSE SO BIG..!
...BARBARA?
IF YOU HURT INSIDE, GET CERTIFIED, AND IF LIFE SHOULD TREAT YOU BAD...
BARBARAAAAAA
DON'T GET EE-EE-EVEN, GET MAD!

BDUMP
DANGEROUS
DO NOT APPROACH
BDUMP
COBBLEPOT
9301
BDUMP
NO
TRUCKS

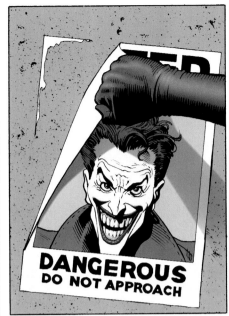

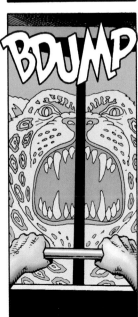

BDUMP
BDUMP
BONUS BROTHERS
CARNIVAL AND
BDUMP
With Compliments

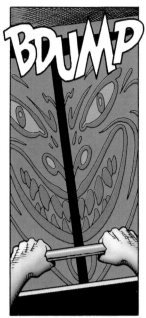

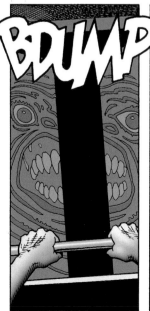

BDUMP

AHH! HERE THEY ARE *NOW!* MY *GOODNESS,* THAT'S *SOME* GHOST-TRAIN...

WHEN THEY WENT *IN,* THE CHAP IN THE *MIDDLE* DIDN'T LOOK A *DAY* OVER *SEVENTEEN,* AND HIS THREE LITTLE *PALS* WERE *PROFESSIONAL BASKETBALL STARS!*

LOOK AT HIM *NOW,* POOR FELLOW. THAT'S WHAT A DOSE OF *REALITY* DOES FOR YOU...

NEVER *TOUCH* THE STUFF *MYSELF,* YOU UNDERSTAND. FIND IT GETS IN THE WAY OF THE *HALLUCINATIONS.*

WHY, *HELLO,* COMMISSIONER! HOW'S *THINGS?*

COMMISSIONER?

HELLO?

ANYBODY *HOME?*

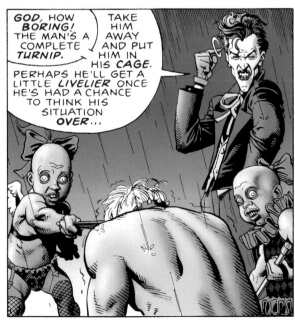

GOD, HOW *BORING!* THE MAN'S A COMPLETE *TURNIP.* PERHAPS HE'LL GET A LITTLE *LIVELIER* ONCE HE'S HAD A CHANCE TO THINK HIS SITUATION *OVER...*

TAKE HIM AWAY AND PUT HIM IN HIS *CAGE.*

..., TO REFLECT UPON *LIFE,* AND ALL ITS RANDOM *INJUSTICE.*

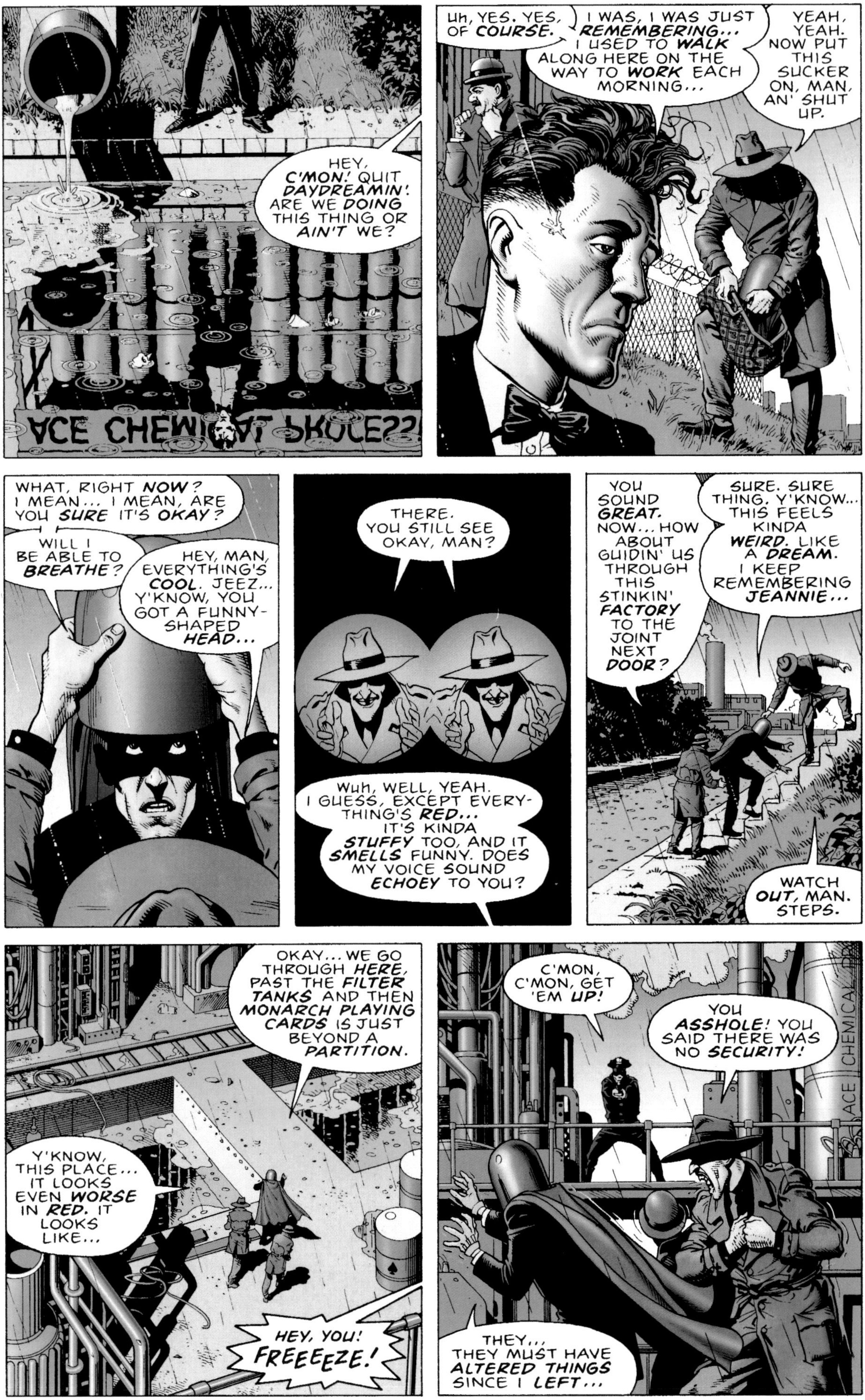
HEY, C'MON! QUIT DAYDREAMIN'. ARE WE DOING THIS THING OR AIN'T WE?
Uh, YES. YES, OF COURSE.
I WAS, I WAS JUST REMEMBERING... I USED TO WALK ALONG HERE ON THE WAY TO WORK EACH MORNING...
YEAH, YEAH. NOW PUT THIS SUCKER ON, MAN, AN' SHUT UP.
WHAT, RIGHT NOW? I MEAN... I MEAN, ARE YOU SURE IT'S OKAY?
WILL I BE ABLE TO BREATHE?
HEY, MAN, EVERYTHING'S COOL. JEEZ... Y'KNOW, YOU GOT A FUNNY-SHAPED HEAD...
THERE. YOU STILL SEE OKAY, MAN?
Wuh, WELL, YEAH. I GUESS, EXCEPT EVERYTHING'S RED... IT'S KINDA STUFFY TOO, AND IT SMELLS FUNNY. DOES MY VOICE SOUND ECHOEY TO YOU?
YOU SOUND GREAT. NOW... HOW ABOUT GUIDIN' US THROUGH THIS STINKIN' FACTORY TO THE JOINT NEXT DOOR?
SURE. SURE THING. Y'KNOW... THIS FEELS KINDA WEIRD. LIKE A DREAM. I KEEP REMEMBERING JEANNIE...
WATCH OUT, MAN. STEPS.
OKAY... WE GO THROUGH HERE, PAST THE FILTER TANKS AND THEN MONARCH PLAYING CARDS IS JUST BEYOND A PARTITION.
Y'KNOW, THIS PLACE... IT LOOKS EVEN WORSE IN RED. IT LOOKS LIKE...
HEY, YOU! FREEEEZE!
C'MON, C'MON, GET 'EM UP!
YOU ASSHOLE! YOU SAID THERE WAS NO SECURITY!
ACE CHEMICAL
THEY... THEY MUST HAVE ALTERED THINGS SINCE I LEFT...

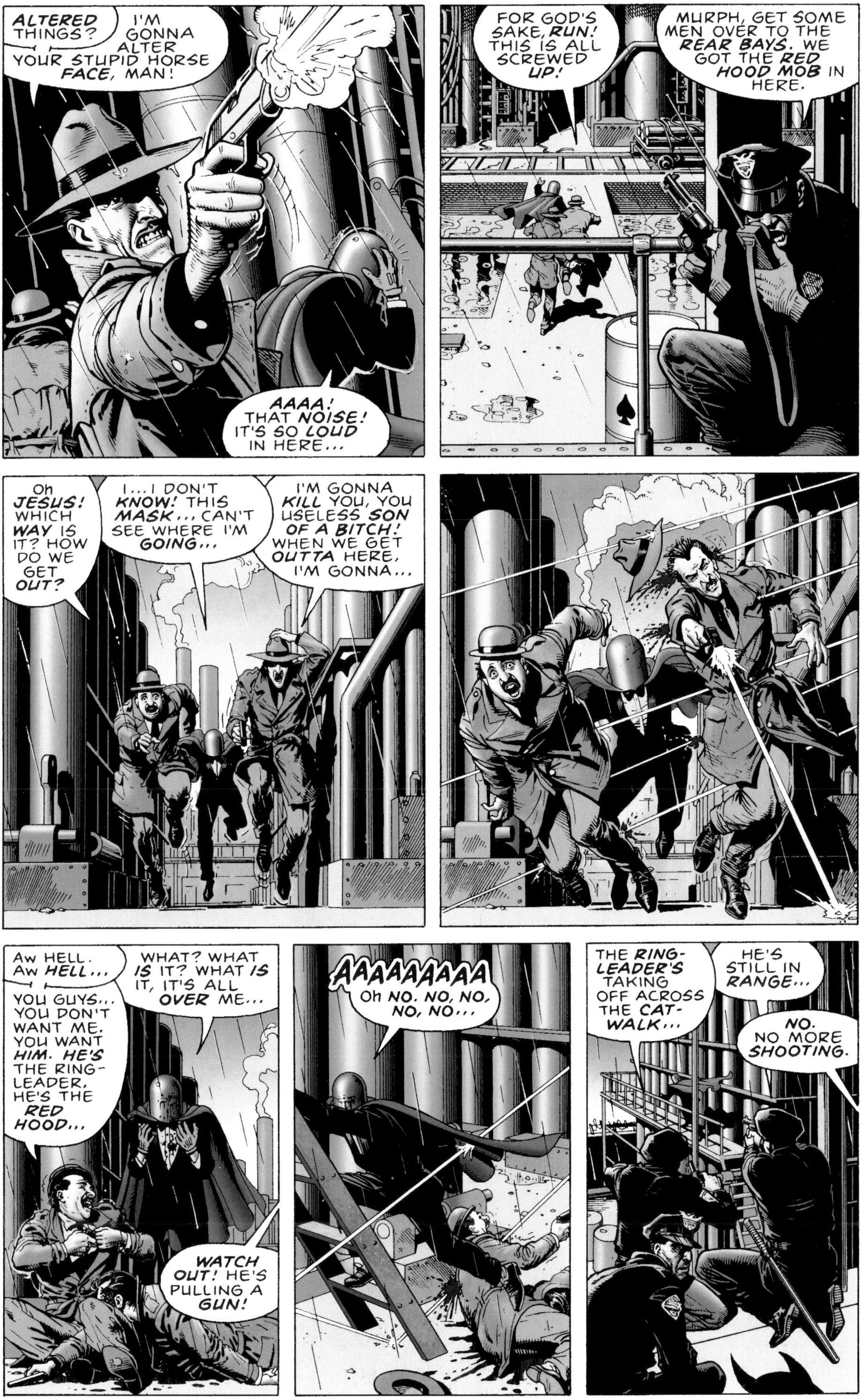
ALTERED THINGS?
I'M GONNA ALTER YOUR STUPID HORSE FACE, MAN!
AAAA! THAT NOISE! IT'S SO LOUD IN HERE...
FOR GOD'S SAKE, RUN! THIS IS ALL SCREWED UP!
MURPH, GET SOME MEN OVER TO THE REAR BAYS. WE GOT THE RED HOOD MOB IN HERE.
Oh JESUS! WHICH WAY IS IT? HOW DO WE GET OUT?
I... I DON'T KNOW! THIS MASK... CAN'T SEE WHERE I'M GOING...
I'M GONNA KILL YOU, YOU USELESS SON OF A BITCH! WHEN WE GET OUTTA HERE, I'M GONNA...
Aw HELL. Aw HELL...
YOU GUYS... YOU DON'T WANT ME. YOU WANT HIM. HE'S THE RING-LEADER. HE'S THE RED HOOD...
WHAT? WHAT IS IT? WHAT IS IT, IT'S ALL OVER ME...
WATCH OUT! HE'S PULLING A GUN!
AAAAAAAAA
Oh NO. NO, NO, NO, NO...
THE RING-LEADER'S TAKING OFF ACROSS THE CAT-WALK...
HE'S STILL IN RANGE...
NO. NO MORE SHOOTING.

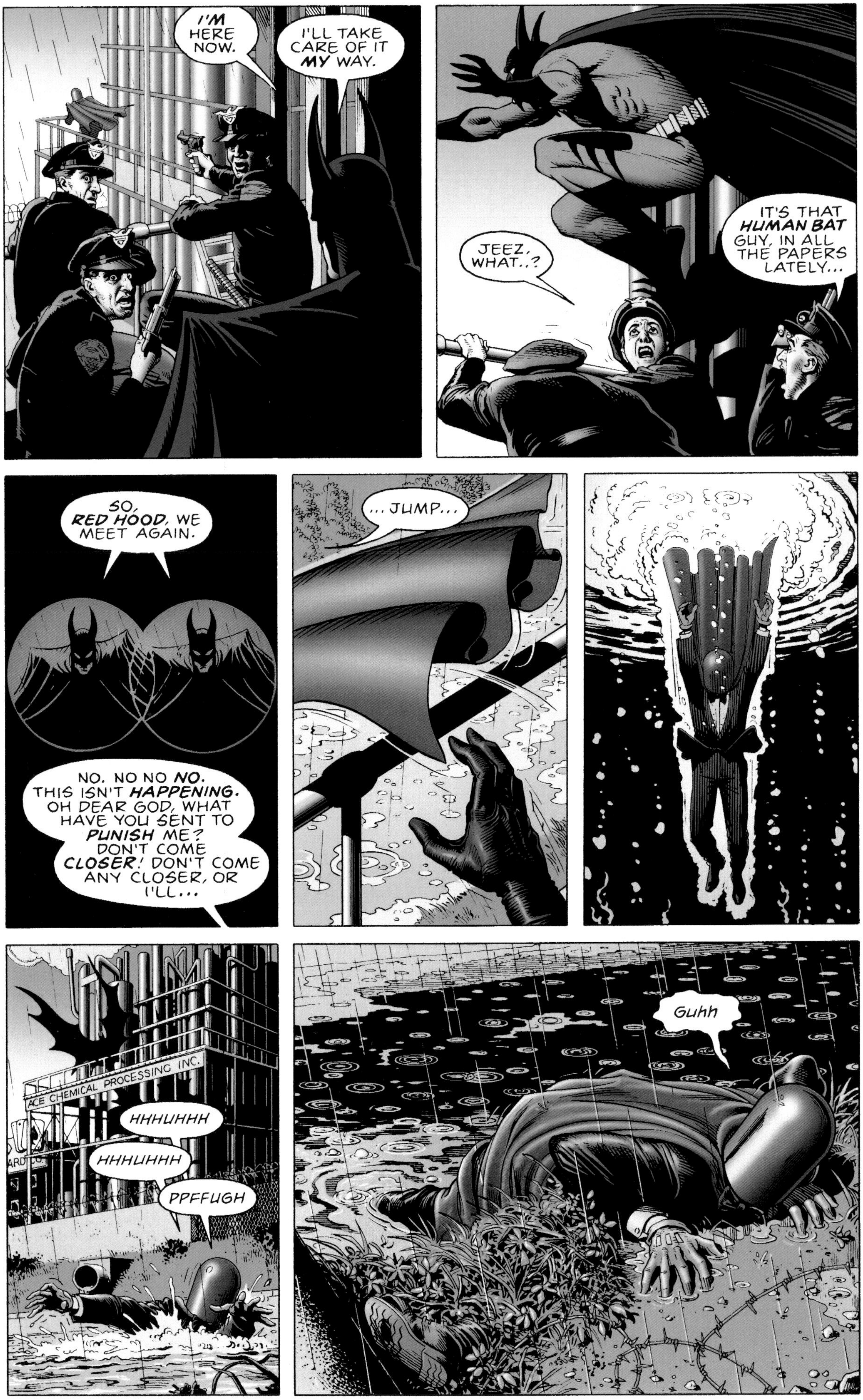
I'M HERE NOW.
I'LL TAKE CARE OF IT MY WAY.
JEEZ, WHAT..?
IT'S THAT HUMAN BAT GUY, IN ALL THE PAPERS LATELY...
SO, RED HOOD, WE MEET AGAIN.
NO. NO NO NO. THIS ISN'T HAPPENING. OH DEAR GOD, WHAT HAVE YOU SENT TO PUNISH ME? DON'T COME CLOSER! DON'T COME ANY CLOSER, OR I'LL...
...JUMP...
ACE CHEMICAL PROCESSING INC.
HHHUHHH
HHHUHHH
PPFFUGH
Guhh

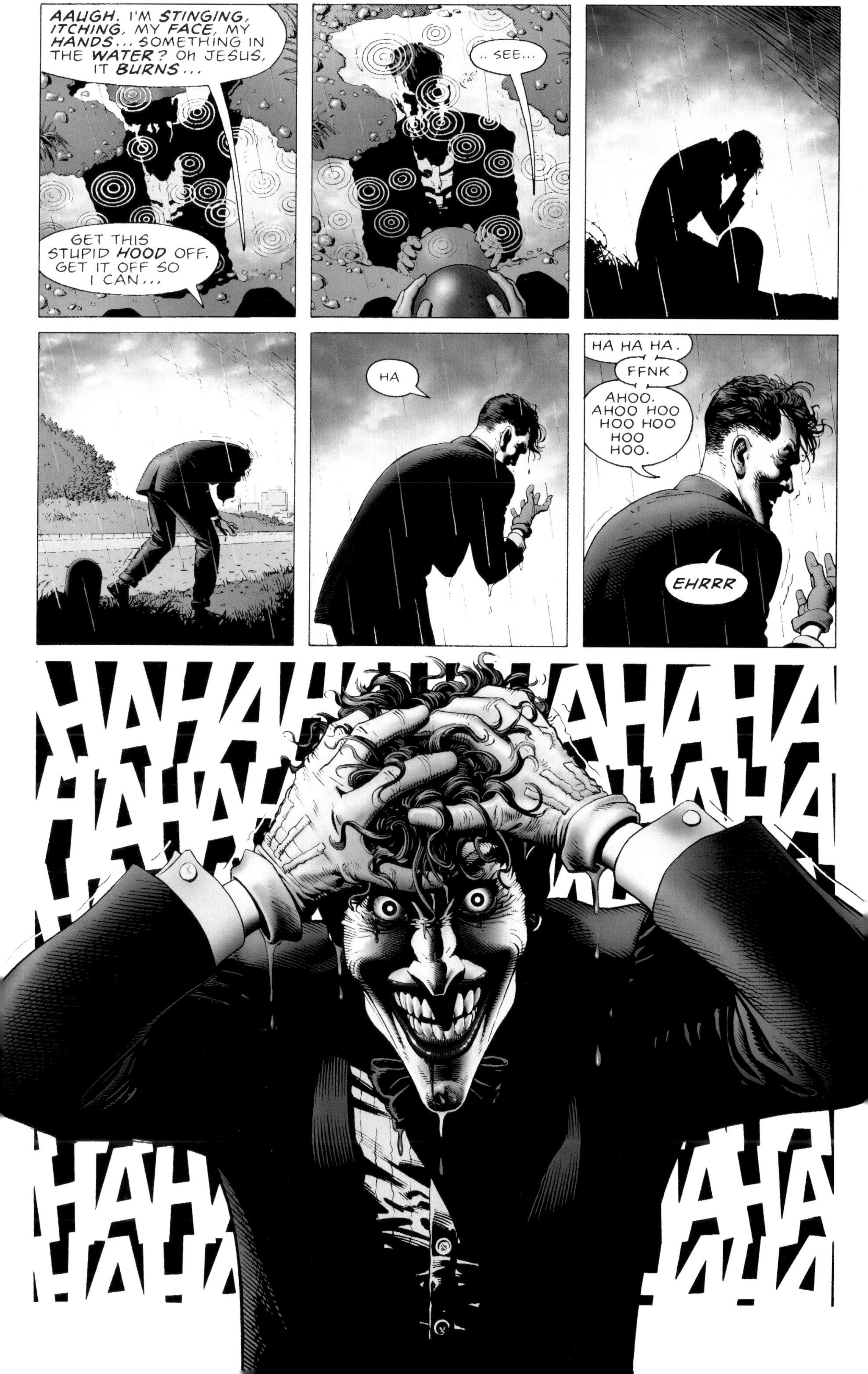
AAUGH. I'M STINGING, ITCHING, MY FACE, MY HANDS... SOMETHING IN THE WATER? Oh JESUS, IT BURNS...
GET THIS STUPID HOOD OFF. GET IT OFF SO I CAN...
.. SEE...
HA
HA HA HA.
FFNK
AHOO. AHOO HOO HOO HOO HOO HOO.
EHRRR
HAHAHAHAHAHA

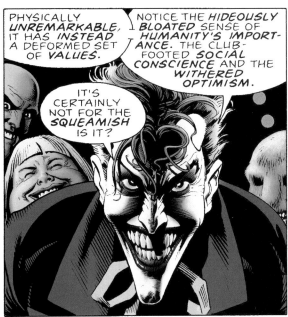

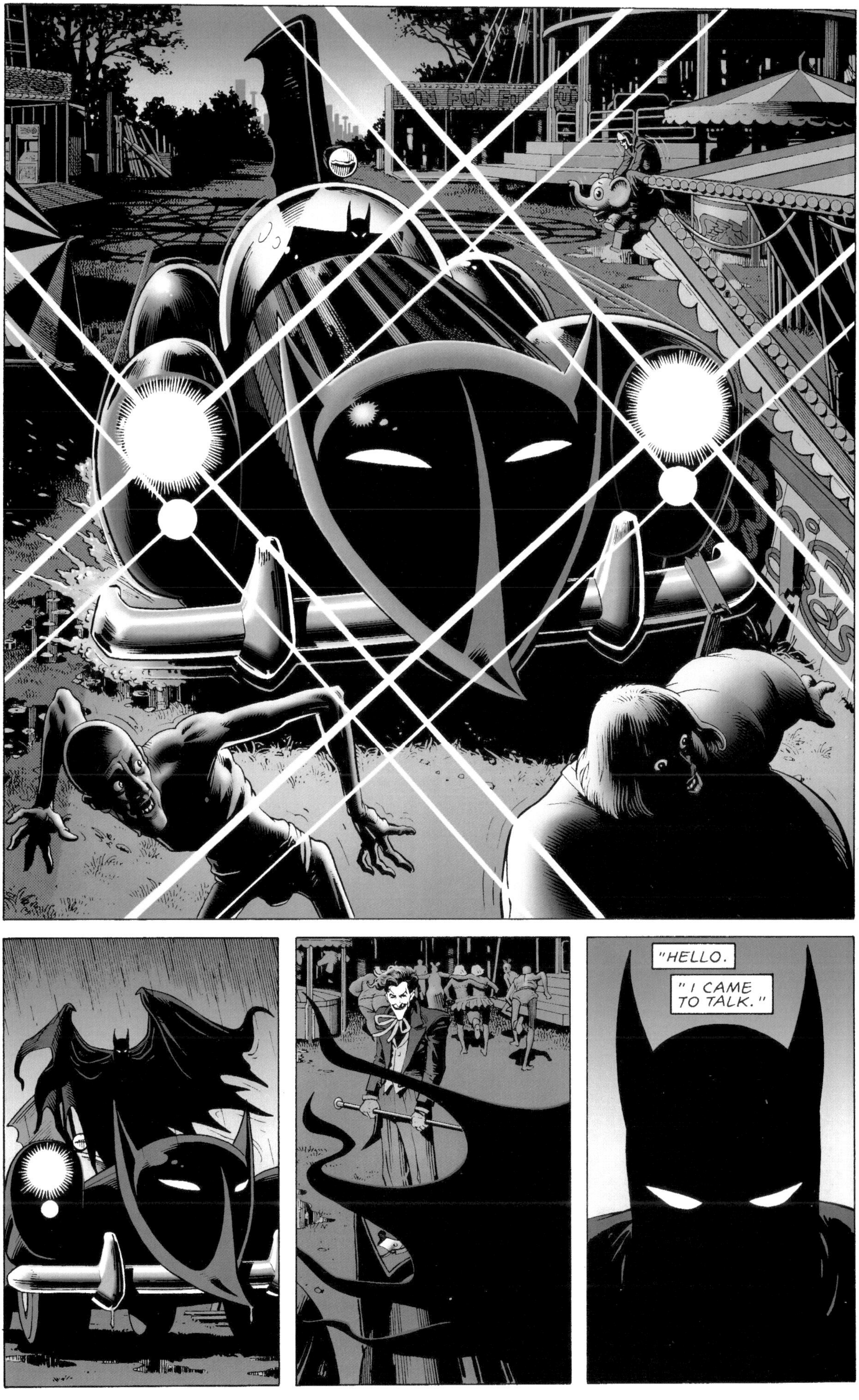
FUN FUN FUN
"HELLO.
"I CAME TO TALK."

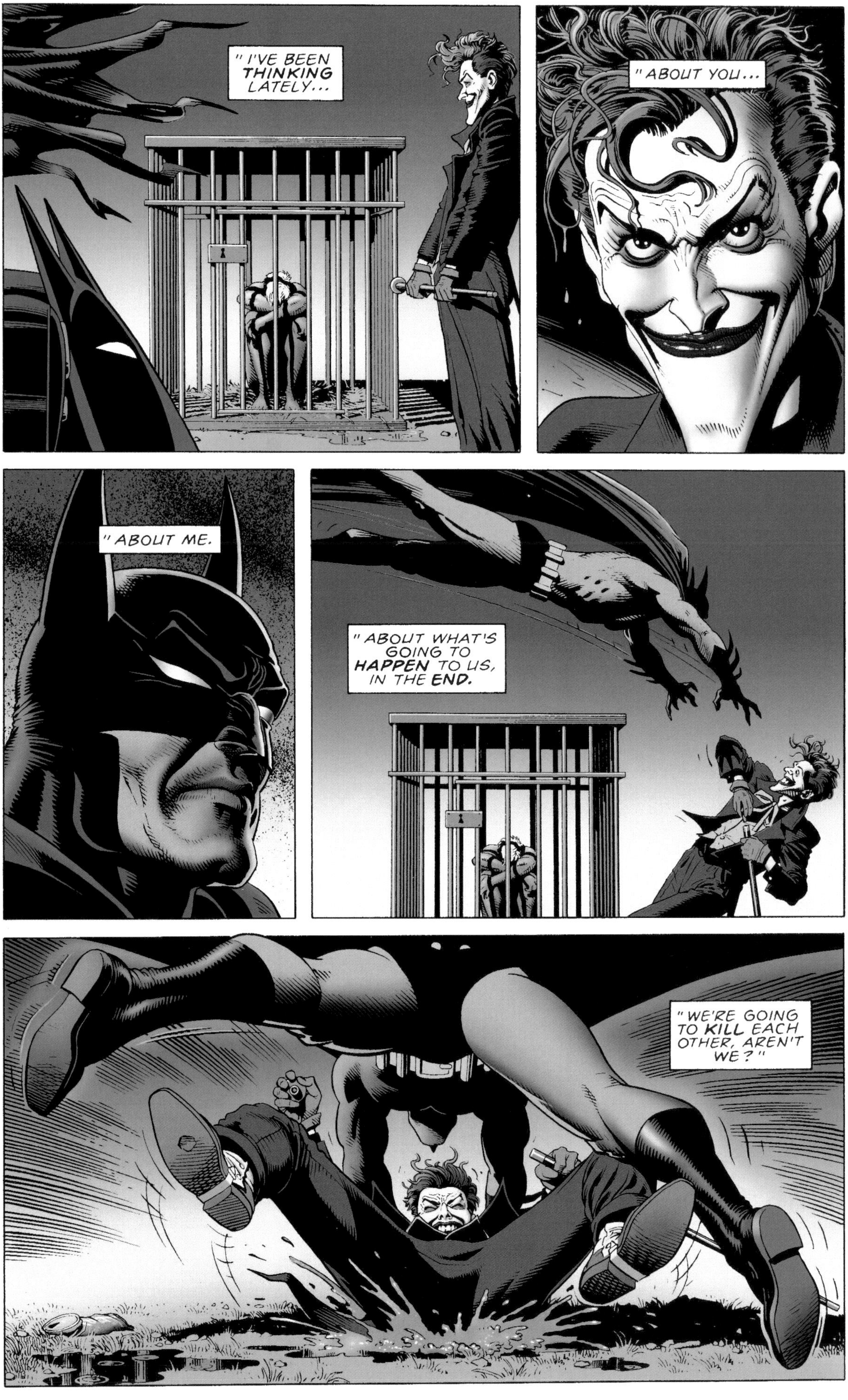
"I'VE BEEN THINKING LATELY...
"ABOUT YOU...
"ABOUT ME.
"ABOUT WHAT'S GOING TO HAPPEN TO US, IN THE END.
"WE'RE GOING TO KILL EACH OTHER, AREN'T WE?"

"PERHAPS YOU'LL KILL ME..."

"PERHAPS I'LL KILL YOU."

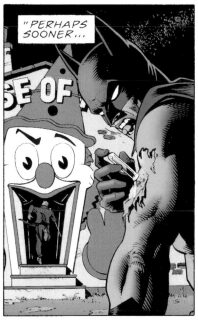

"PERHAPS SOONER..."

"PERHAPS LATER."

BUMP

JIM?

JIM, ARE YOU... ARE YOU STILL OKAY?

OH GOD. AHUHUHUHUHUH. OH GODDDDD...

IT'S OKAY. LET IT COME.

HE... HE SHOT *BARBARA.* SHOWED ME PH- *PHOTO-GRAPHS...*

HE TRIED TO DRIVE ME *MAD.*

LISTEN, THE *POLICE* ARE FOLLOWING RIGHT *BEHIND* ME...

I'LL STAY HERE WITH YOU UNTIL THEY *ARRIVE.*

NO! NO, I'M *OKAY!* YOU HAVE TO GO AFTER *HIM!*

I WANT HIM *BROUGHT IN...*

...AND I WANT HIM BROUGHT IN BY THE *BOOK!*

I'LL DO MY BEST.

BY THE *BOOK,* YOU *HEAR?*

WE HAVE TO *SHOW* HIM!

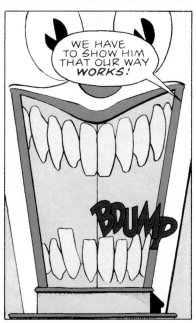

WE HAVE TO SHOW HIM THAT OUR WAY *WORKS!*

BDUMP

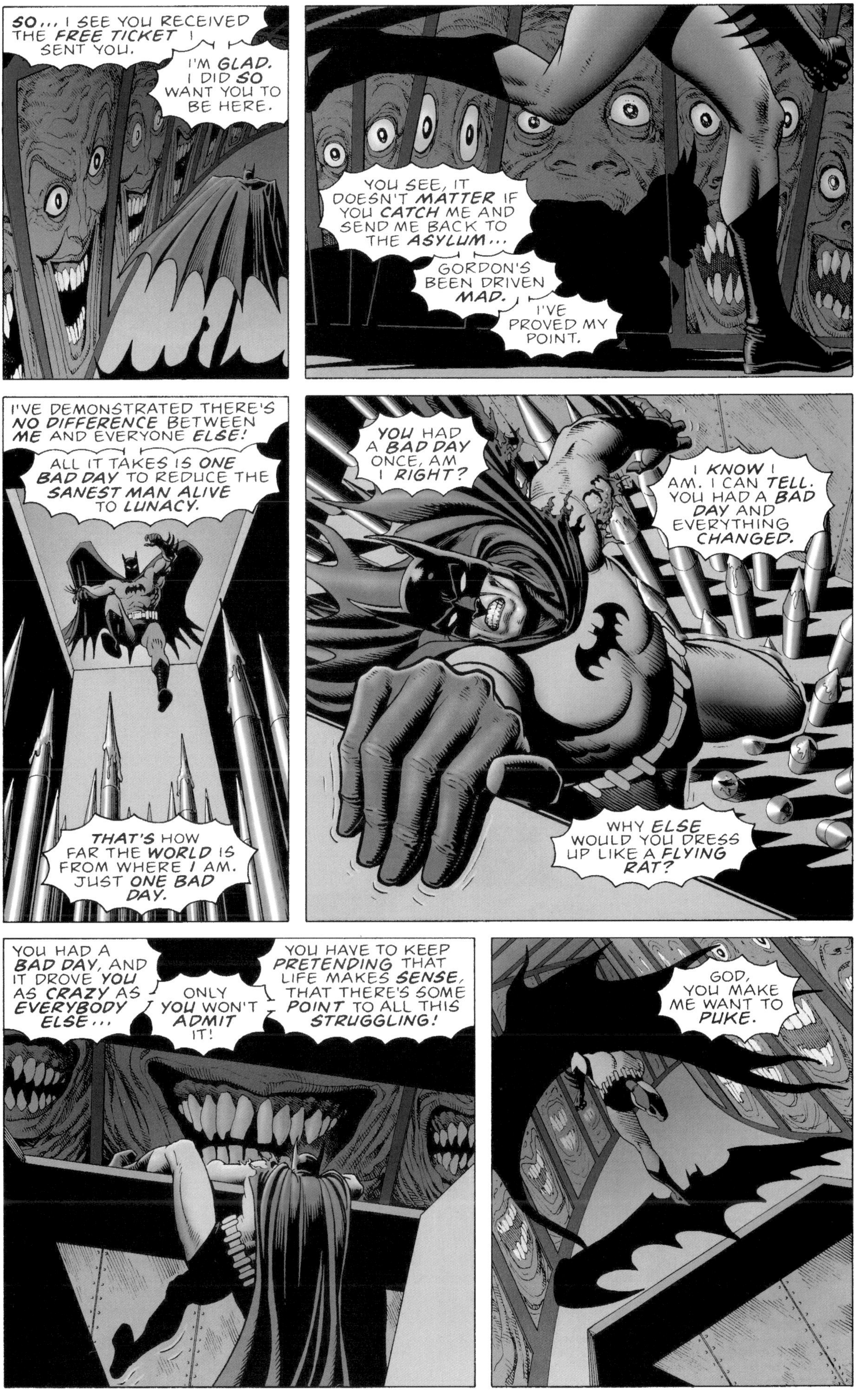
SO... I SEE YOU RECEIVED THE FREE TICKET I SENT YOU.
I'M GLAD. I DID SO WANT YOU TO BE HERE.
YOU SEE, IT DOESN'T MATTER IF YOU CATCH ME AND SEND ME BACK TO THE ASYLUM...
GORDON'S BEEN DRIVEN MAD.
I'VE PROVED MY POINT.
I'VE DEMONSTRATED THERE'S NO DIFFERENCE BETWEEN ME AND EVERYONE ELSE!
ALL IT TAKES IS ONE BAD DAY TO REDUCE THE SANEST MAN ALIVE TO LUNACY.
THAT'S HOW FAR THE WORLD IS FROM WHERE I AM. JUST ONE BAD DAY.
YOU HAD A BAD DAY ONCE, AM I RIGHT?
I KNOW I AM. I CAN TELL. YOU HAD A BAD DAY AND EVERYTHING CHANGED.
WHY ELSE WOULD YOU DRESS UP LIKE A FLYING RAT?
YOU HAD A BAD DAY, AND IT DROVE YOU AS CRAZY AS EVERYBODY ELSE...
ONLY YOU WON'T ADMIT IT!
YOU HAVE TO KEEP PRETENDING THAT LIFE MAKES SENSE, THAT THERE'S SOME POINT TO ALL THIS STRUGGLING!
GOD, YOU MAKE ME WANT TO PUKE.

I *MEAN*, WHAT *IS* IT WITH YOU? WHAT *MADE* YOU WHAT YOU *ARE*?

GIRLFRIEND KILLED BY THE *MOB*, MAYBE? *BROTHER* CARVED UP BY SOME *MUGGER*?

SOME-THING LIKE THAT, I BET. *SOMETHING* LIKE THAT...

SOMETHING LIKE THAT HAPPENED TO *ME*, YOU KNOW. I... I'M NOT EXACTLY *SURE* WHAT IT WAS. SOME-TIMES I REMEMBER IT ONE WAY, SOMETIMES *ANOTHER*...

IF I'M GOING TO HAVE A *PAST*, I PREFER IT TO BE *MULTIPLE CHOICE*! HA HA HA!

BUT *MY* POINT IS... MY POINT *IS*, I WENT *CRAZY*.

WHEN I *SAW* WHAT A BLACK, AWFUL *JOKE* THE WORLD *WAS*, I WENT CRAZY AS A *COOT*! I ADMIT IT!

WHY CAN'T *YOU*?

I MEAN, YOU'RE NOT *UNINTELLIGENT*! YOU *MUST* SEE THE *REALITY* OF THE SITUATION.

DO YOU *KNOW* HOW MANY TIMES WE'VE COME CLOSE TO *WORLD WAR THREE* OVER A FLOCK OF *GEESE* ON A *COMPUTER SCREEN*?

ALL OF MIRRO

DO YOU KNOW WHAT TRIGGERED THE *LAST* WORLD WAR? AN ARGUMENT OVER HOW MANY *TELEGRAPH POLES* GERMANY OWED ITS *WAR DEBT* CREDITORS!

TELEGRAPH POLES! HA HA HA HA HA *HA*!

IT'S ALL A *JOKE*! EVERYTHING ANYBODY EVER *VALUED* OR *STRUGGLED* FOR... IT'S ALL A *MONSTROUS*, DEMENTED *GAG*!

SO WHY CAN'T YOU SEE THE *FUNNY* SIDE?

WHY AREN'T YOU *LAUGHING*?

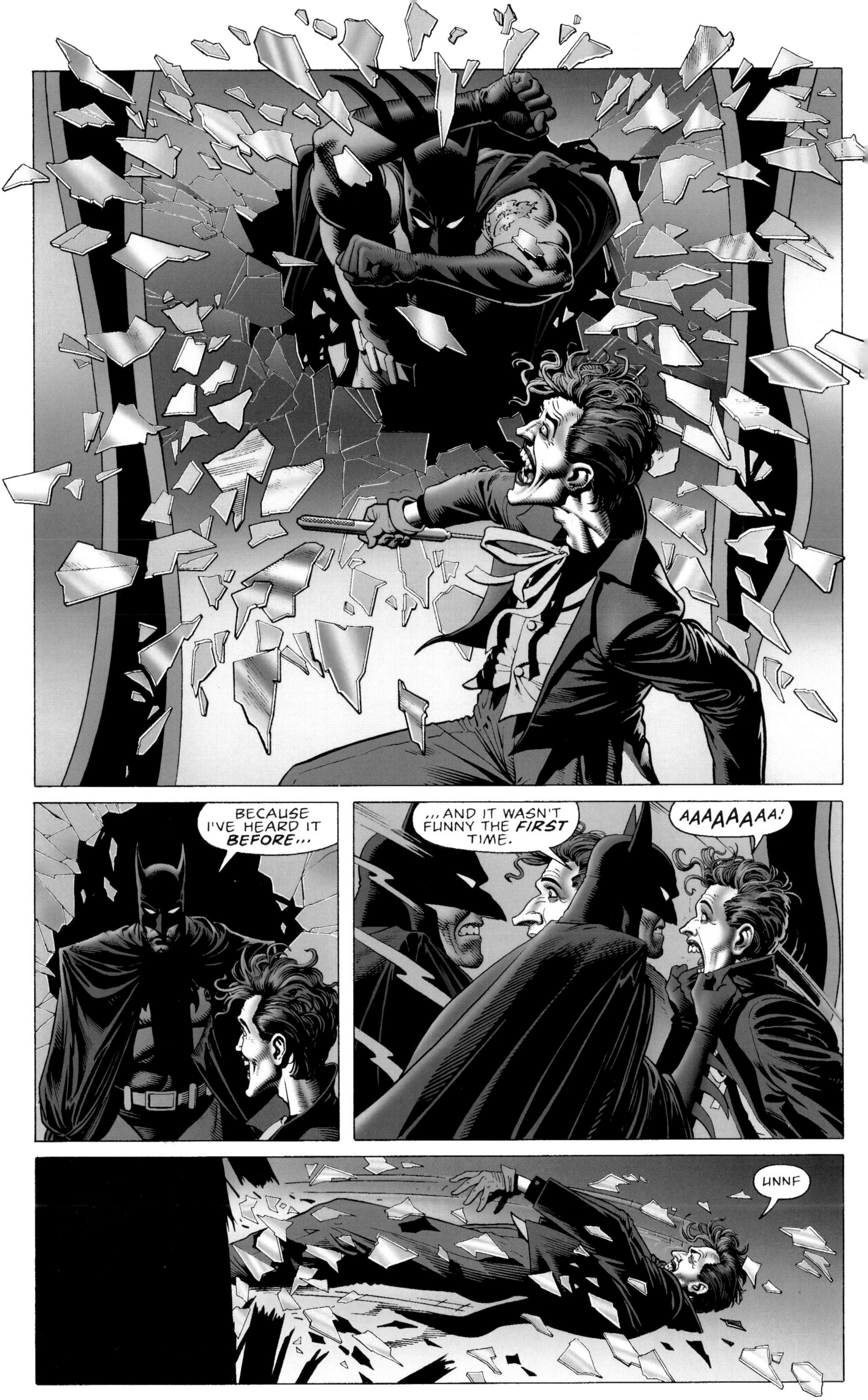
BECAUSE I'VE HEARD IT BEFORE...
...AND IT WASN'T FUNNY THE FIRST TIME.
AAAAAAAA!
UNNF

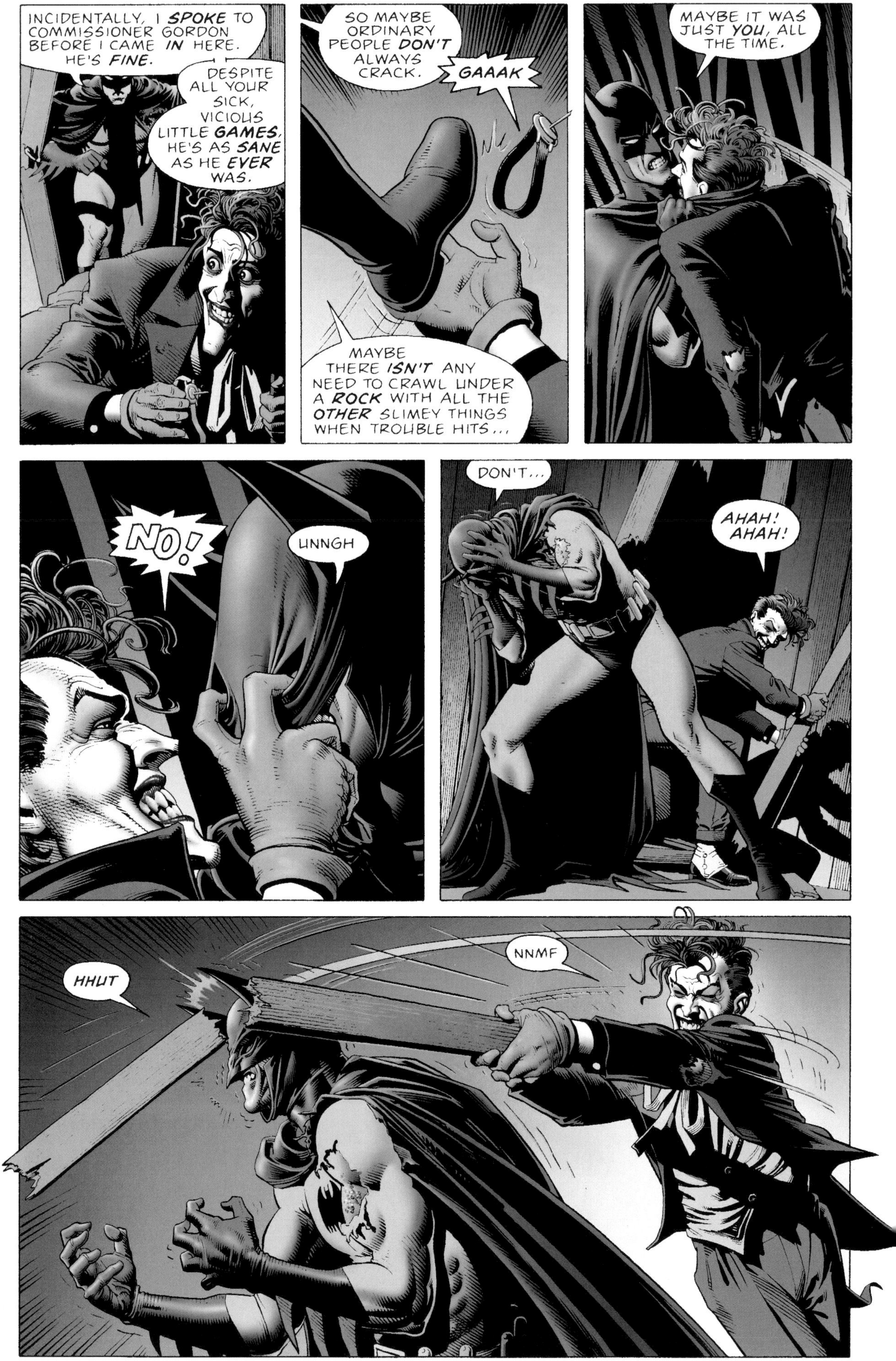
INCIDENTALLY, I SPOKE TO COMMISSIONER GORDON BEFORE I CAME IN HERE. HE'S FINE.
DESPITE ALL YOUR SICK, VICIOUS LITTLE GAMES, HE'S AS SANE AS HE EVER WAS.
SO MAYBE ORDINARY PEOPLE DON'T ALWAYS CRACK.
GAAAK
MAYBE THERE ISN'T ANY NEED TO CRAWL UNDER A ROCK WITH ALL THE OTHER SLIMEY THINGS WHEN TROUBLE HITS...
MAYBE IT WAS JUST YOU, ALL THE TIME.
NO!
UNNGH
DON'T...
AHAH! AHAH!
HHUT
NNMF

GNUHHH...

PTCHIK!

UOAA

HOOOF

FUHHH...

BDUMP

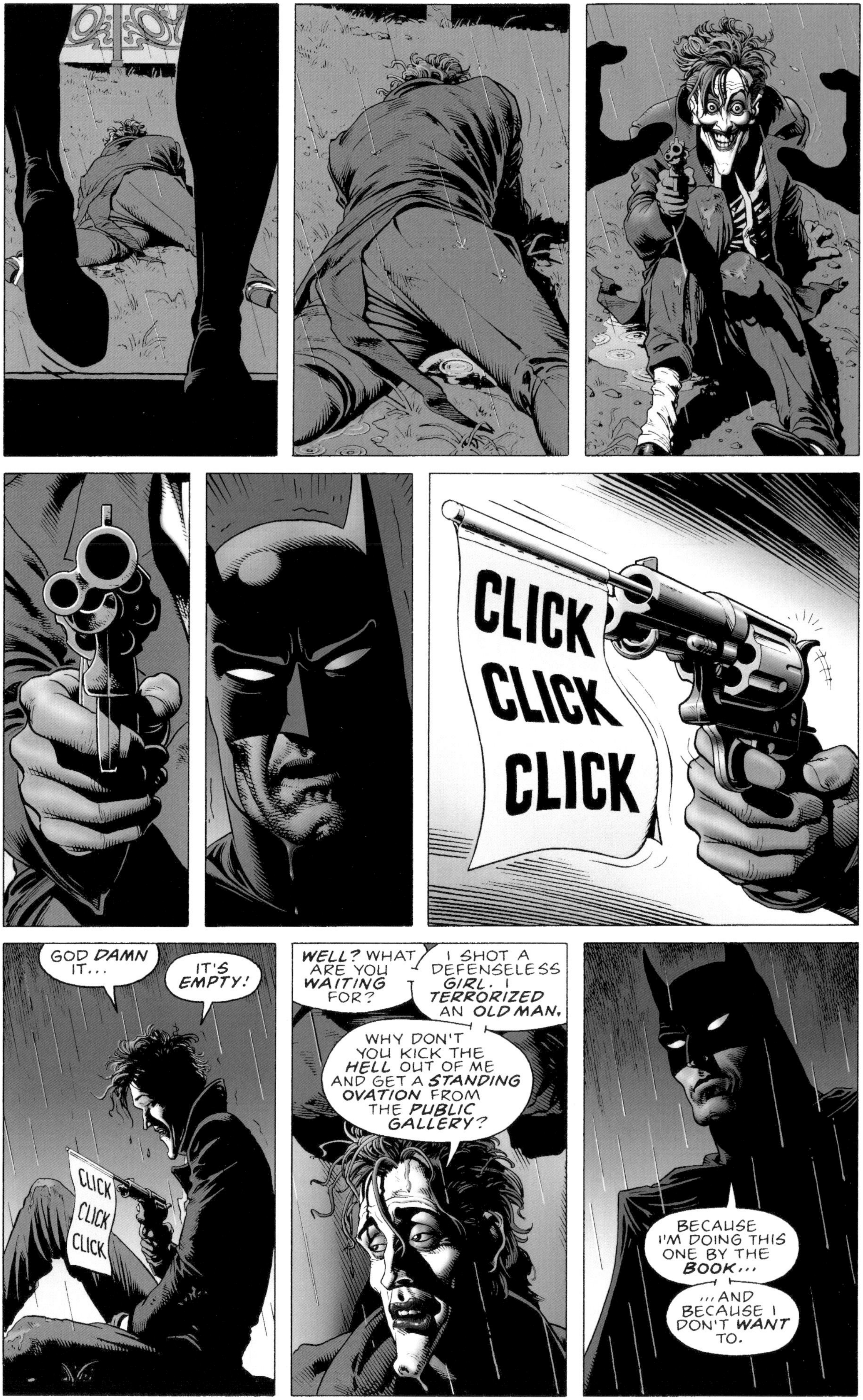
CLICK
CLICK
CLICK
GOD DAMN IT...
IT'S EMPTY!
CLICK
CLICK
CLICK
WELL? WHAT ARE YOU WAITING FOR?
I SHOT A DEFENSELESS GIRL. I TERRORIZED AN OLD MAN.
WHY DON'T YOU KICK THE HELL OUT OF ME AND GET A STANDING OVATION FROM THE PUBLIC GALLERY?
BECAUSE I'M DOING THIS ONE BY THE BOOK...
...AND BECAUSE I DON'T WANT TO.

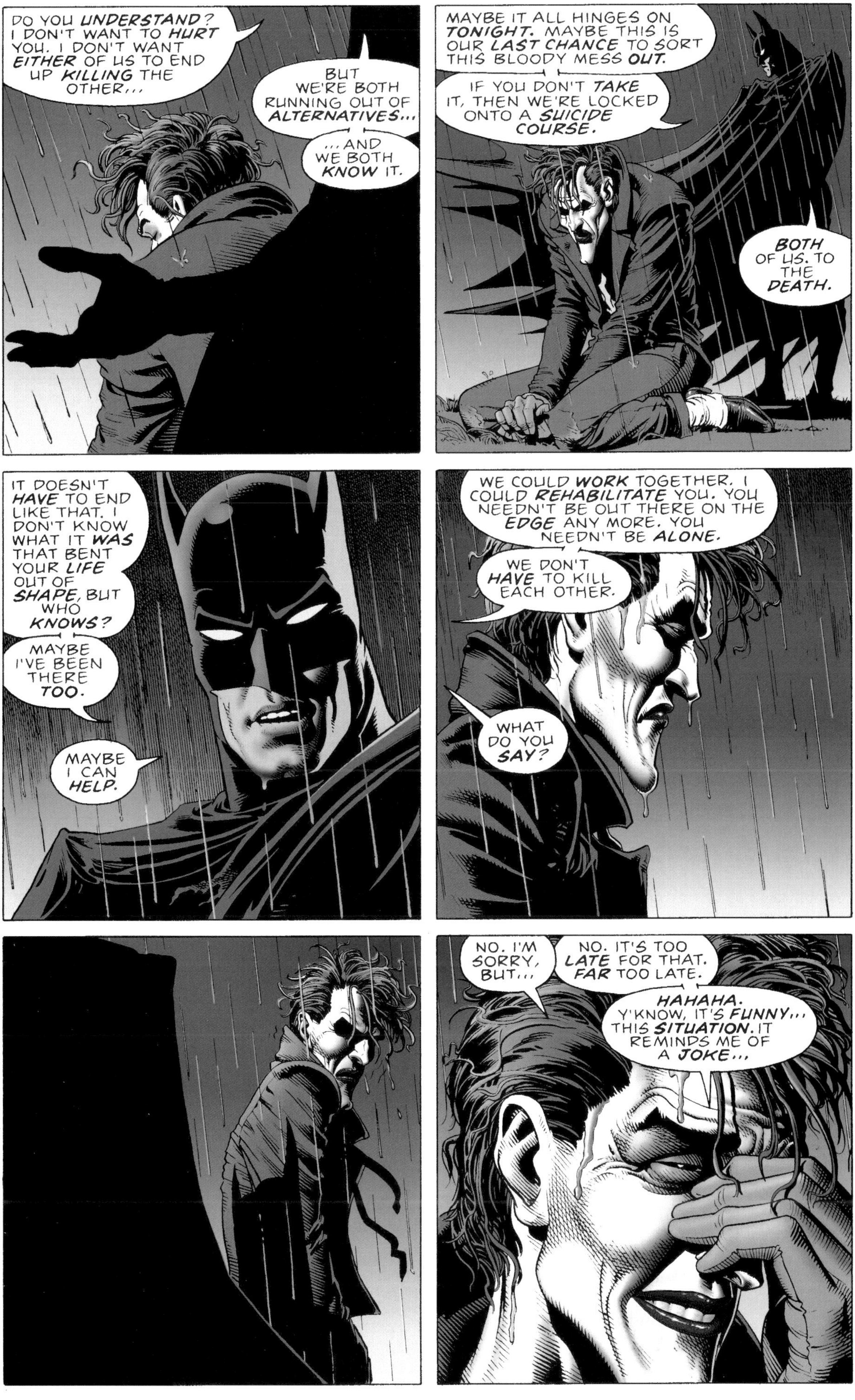
DO YOU UNDERSTAND? I DON'T WANT TO HURT YOU. I DON'T WANT EITHER OF US TO END UP KILLING THE OTHER...
BUT WE'RE BOTH RUNNING OUT OF ALTERNATIVES...
...AND WE BOTH KNOW IT.
MAYBE IT ALL HINGES ON TONIGHT. MAYBE THIS IS OUR LAST CHANCE TO SORT THIS BLOODY MESS OUT.
IF YOU DON'T TAKE IT, THEN WE'RE LOCKED ONTO A SUICIDE COURSE.
BOTH OF US. TO THE DEATH.
IT DOESN'T HAVE TO END LIKE THAT. I DON'T KNOW WHAT IT WAS THAT BENT YOUR LIFE OUT OF SHAPE, BUT WHO KNOWS?
MAYBE I'VE BEEN THERE TOO.
MAYBE I CAN HELP.
WE COULD WORK TOGETHER. I COULD REHABILITATE YOU. YOU NEEDN'T BE OUT THERE ON THE EDGE ANY MORE. YOU NEEDN'T BE ALONE.
WE DON'T HAVE TO KILL EACH OTHER.
WHAT DO YOU SAY?
NO. I'M SORRY, BUT...
NO. IT'S TOO LATE FOR THAT. FAR TOO LATE.
HAHAHA. Y'KNOW, IT'S FUNNY... THIS SITUATION. IT REMINDS ME OF A JOKE...

SEE, THERE WERE THESE TWO GUYS IN A *LUNATIC ASYLUM...*

...AND *ONE* NIGHT, ONE NIGHT THEY DECIDE THEY DON'T *LIKE* LIVING IN AN *ASYLUM* ANY MORE.

THEY DECIDE THEY'RE GOING TO *ESCAPE!*

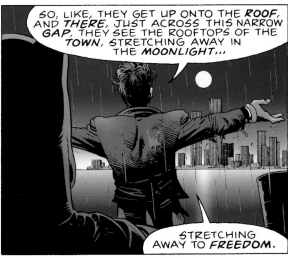

SO, LIKE, THEY GET UP ONTO THE *ROOF,* AND *THERE,* JUST ACROSS THIS NARROW *GAP,* THEY SEE THE ROOFTOPS OF THE *TOWN,* STRETCHING AWAY IN THE *MOONLIGHT...*

STRETCHING AWAY TO *FREEDOM.*

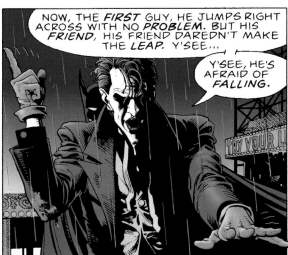

NOW, THE *FIRST* GUY, HE JUMPS RIGHT ACROSS WITH NO *PROBLEM.* BUT HIS *FRIEND,* HIS FRIEND DAREDN'T MAKE THE *LEAP.* Y'SEE...

Y'SEE, HE'S AFRAID OF *FALLING.*

SO THEN, THE *FIRST* GUY HAS AN *IDEA...*

HE SAYS "*HEY!* I HAVE MY *FLASHLIGHT* WITH ME! I'LL SHINE IT ACROSS THE *GAP* BETWEEN THE *BUILDINGS.* YOU CAN WALK ALONG THE *BEAM* AND *JOIN* ME!"

B-BUT THE *SECOND* GUY JUST SHAKES HIS *HEAD.*

HE SUH-SAYS...

HE SAYS "WH-WHAT DO YOU THINK I *AM? CRAZY?"*

"YOU'D TURN IT *OFF* WHEN I WAS HALF WAY *ACROSS!"*

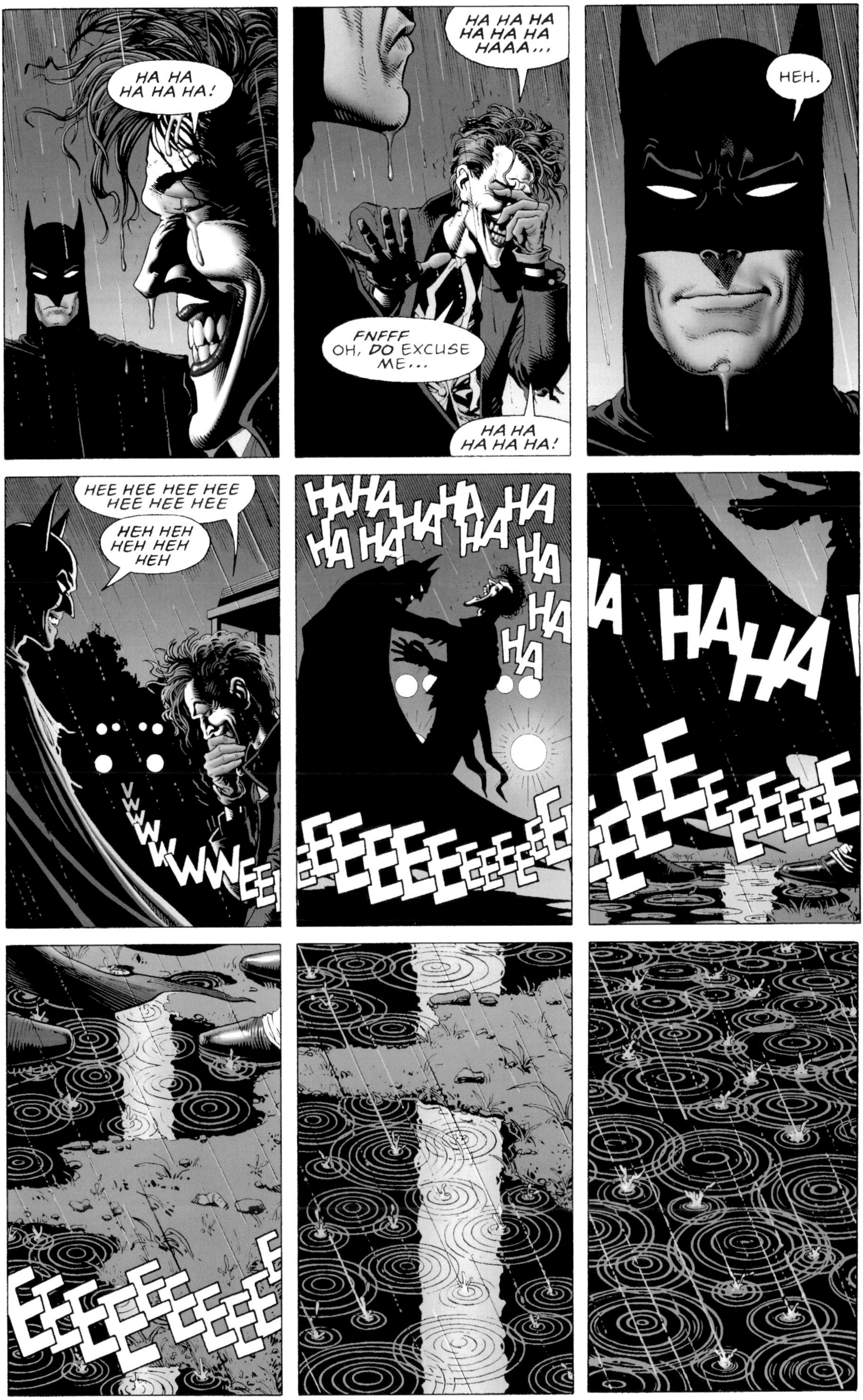
HA HA HA HA HA!
HA HA HA HA HA HA HAAA...
FNFFF OH, DO EXCUSE ME...
HA HA HA HA HA!
HEH.
HEE HEE HEE HEE HEE HEE HEE
HEH HEH HEH HEH HEH

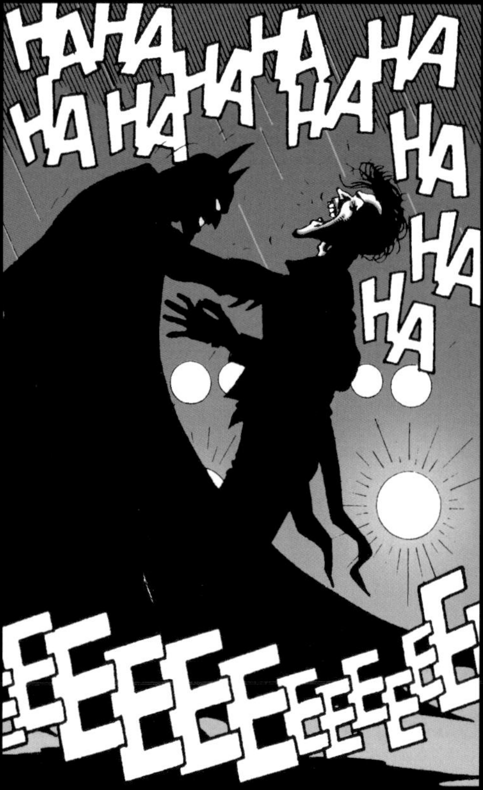
HA HA HA HA HA
HA HA HA HA HA
HA
HA
HA
HA
EEEEEEEEEEEE

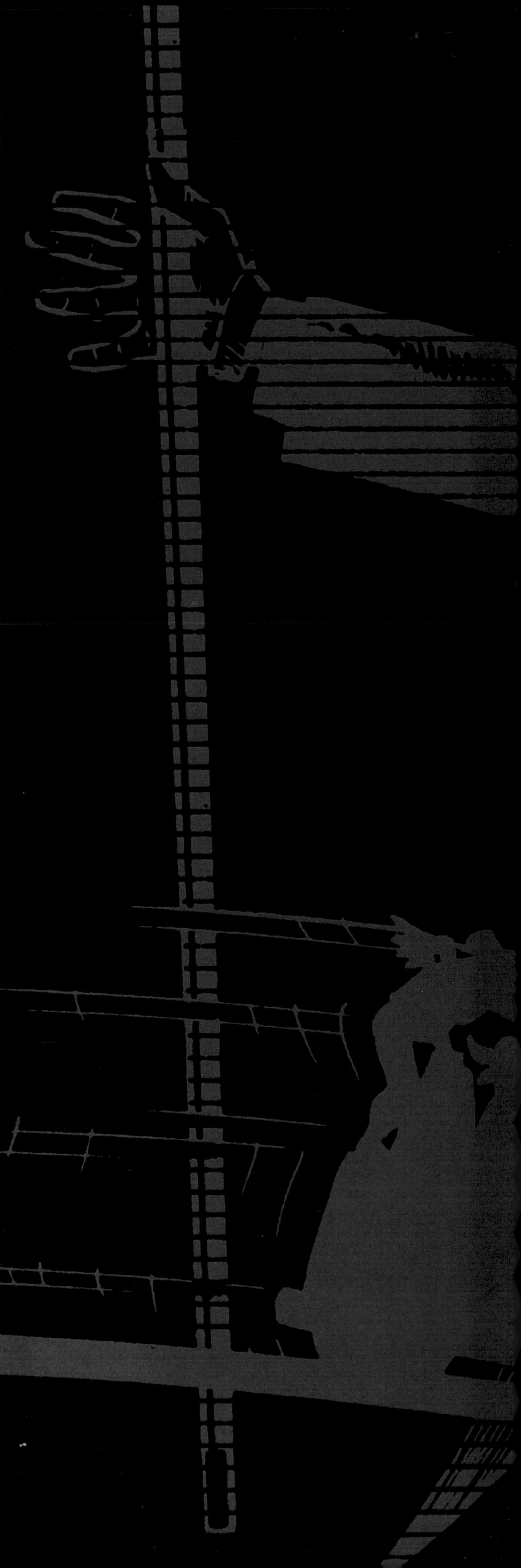

A F T E R W O R D

I've been asked to write the "afterword" to this book — or should that be the "in between"? I'm told by my editor Bob Harras that there's room for up to 800 words. If I go on longer we have to start dropping pages of art and we wouldn't want that, would we? So, reader, if I should stop in mid-sentence it's because I've run out of space.

I've just read Tim Sale's generous introduction. Of all the introductions I've ever received, it's without doubt the most....recent. Having just sat with my 11-year old son watching the hit TV show *Heroes,* it's pretty cool being introduced by its star artist. It seems additionally cool to me that all the writing in this book has been given over not to writers but to artists, a breed of people not known for their ability to string a sentence together — but so far so good.

There's a minor detail that Tim got wrong, actually. It was me that asked Alan to write the book and not the other way round. THE KILLING JOKE was not a project instigated by Alan, nor was it, as far as I know, a labor of love for him, and it doesn't usually appear in a list of his greatest works. I was glad he agreed to write it, though. At the time we'd known each other for quite a while and narrowly missed working together a couple of times. In a peculiar form of homage to him I haven't drawn a comic book story written by any other writer in the last 22 years. When you've worked with the best, anything else would seem like a backward step.

The script for THE KILLING JOKE was very good, but I must admit I had to grit my teeth a couple of times during the drawing of it. I, for instance, would never have chosen to reveal a Joker origin. I think of this as just one of a number of possible origin stories manifesting itself in the Joker's fevered brain. Also, I wouldn't have done such terrible harm to poor Barbara. The story, though, does contain some great iconic moments, my favorite being the scene when the Joker discovers that the gun — as far as we know the same one that maimed Barbara — is empty. People seemed to find the last page of the story ambiguous, so before I conclude this text, remind me to reveal what actually happened.

The most notable absentee from this edition is THE KILLING JOKE's original colorist, John Higgins, and I want to thank him for jumping in when he did and finishing the book so promptly. Back in the pre-computer days of "blue line," airbrush and poster colors, even though I had specific views on how I wanted it to look, I wouldn't have been able to color it myself. It's probably well known that John's choice of colors turned out to be startlingly at odds with what I had in mind so, in February 2007, when Bob Harras told me about this edition, I said, "PLEASE can I recolor the whole thing?"

Technical wizard Jeb Woodard sent me files of the line art which, through some computer alchemy only he understands, he'd isolated from the printed color pages — the original KILLING JOKE artwork has long since disappeared into the hands of collectors — and as I got on with the coloring process on my Mac it was tempting and easy to make changes to the line art itself — a bit of feathering here, a completely redrawn face there. The eagle-eyed may notice that every page has something slightly different on it from THE KILLING JOKE of 20 years ago. There's at least one figure that wasn't there the first time around. Think of it as a Spot-the-Difference book.

"An Innocent Guy" (that's what it's called even though it doesn't say so on it) is of special significance to me. As I became less inclined to work with writers or colorists it was particularly tempting to write a Batman story that was, for better or worse, completely by me. It gave me the opportunity to draw all the scenes I hadn't had a chance to draw in THE KILLING JOKE, including my homage to the unsettlingly surreal Dick Sprang-era Batman that I loved as a kid but combine it with a darker, more morally ambiguous theme that I'd stolen shamelessly from other sources. In so doing I managed to upset at least one mother of a seven-year-old boy who wrote me a letter of protest. Jeb supervised the meticulous painting out of the Zipatone that covered the artwork for the original black and white printing (he didn't quite get it all. You'll see bits of it lingering here and there) and I colored it up for the first time ever. I hope you enjoy these and the preceding 46 pages.

Speaking of which, it's time I revealed what really happened at the end of THE KILLING JOKE: as our protagonists stood there in the rain laughing at the final joke, the police lights reflecting in the pools of filthy water underfoot, the Batman's hand reached out and......

Brian Bolland

Not far from Six Mile Bottom, UK 2008

Writer & Illustrator: Brian Bolland

Letterer: Ellie DeVille

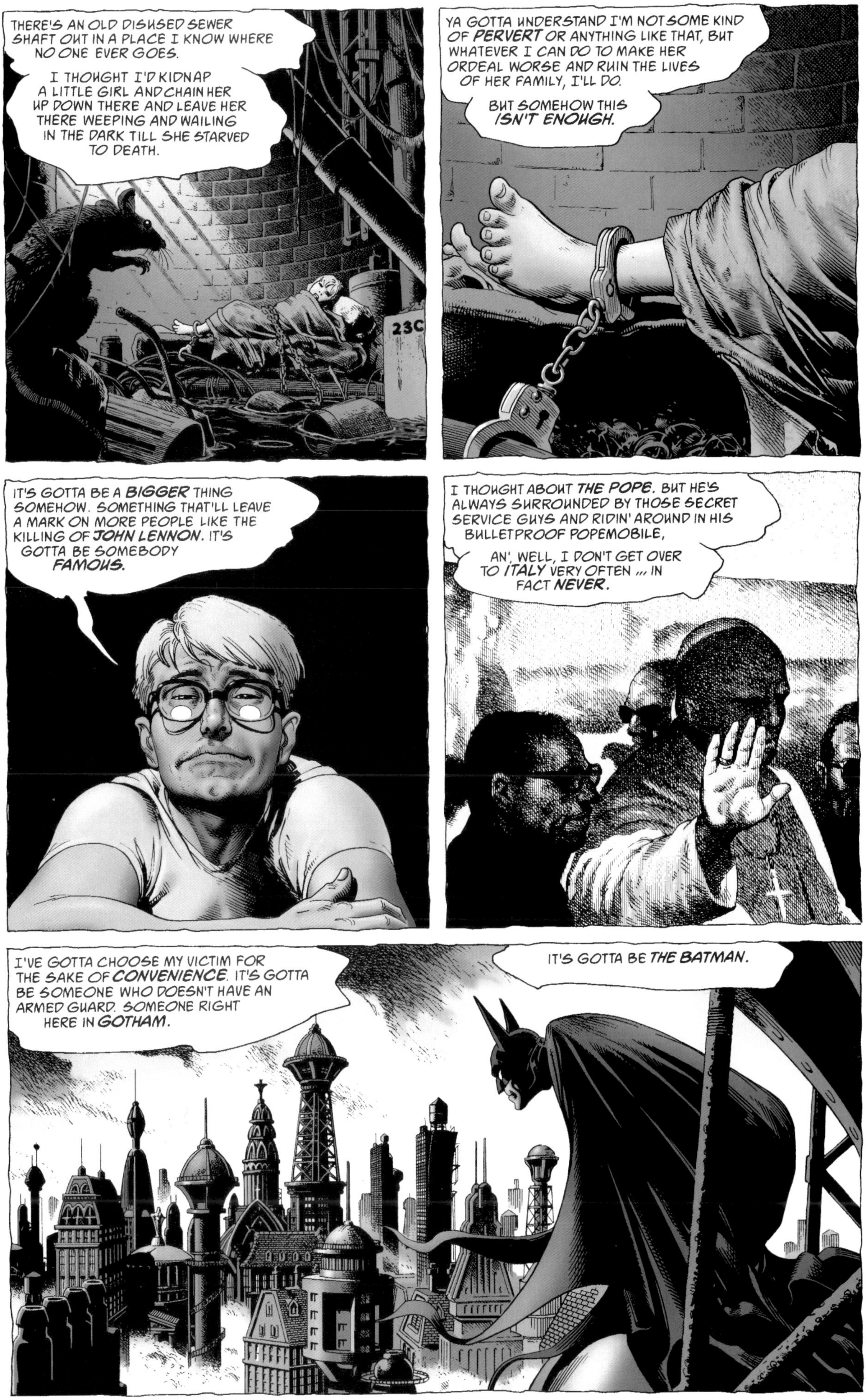
THERE'S AN OLD DISUSED SEWER SHAFT OUT IN A PLACE I KNOW WHERE NO ONE EVER GOES.
I THOUGHT I'D KIDNAP A LITTLE GIRL AND CHAIN HER UP DOWN THERE AND LEAVE HER THERE WEEPING AND WAILING IN THE DARK TILL SHE STARVED TO DEATH.
23C
YA GOTTA UNDERSTAND I'M NOT SOME KIND OF PERVERT OR ANYTHING LIKE THAT, BUT WHATEVER I CAN DO TO MAKE HER ORDEAL WORSE AND RUIN THE LIVES OF HER FAMILY, I'LL DO.
BUT SOMEHOW THIS ISN'T ENOUGH.
IT'S GOTTA BE A BIGGER THING SOMEHOW. SOMETHING THAT'LL LEAVE A MARK ON MORE PEOPLE LIKE THE KILLING OF JOHN LENNON. IT'S GOTTA BE SOMEBODY FAMOUS.
I THOUGHT ABOUT THE POPE. BUT HE'S ALWAYS SURROUNDED BY THOSE SECRET SERVICE GUYS AND RIDIN' AROUND IN HIS BULLETPROOF POPEMOBILE,
AN', WELL, I DON'T GET OVER TO ITALY VERY OFTEN ... IN FACT NEVER.
I'VE GOTTA CHOOSE MY VICTIM FOR THE SAKE OF CONVENIENCE. IT'S GOTTA BE SOMEONE WHO DOESN'T HAVE AN ARMED GUARD. SOMEONE RIGHT HERE IN GOTHAM.
IT'S GOTTA BE THE BATMAN.

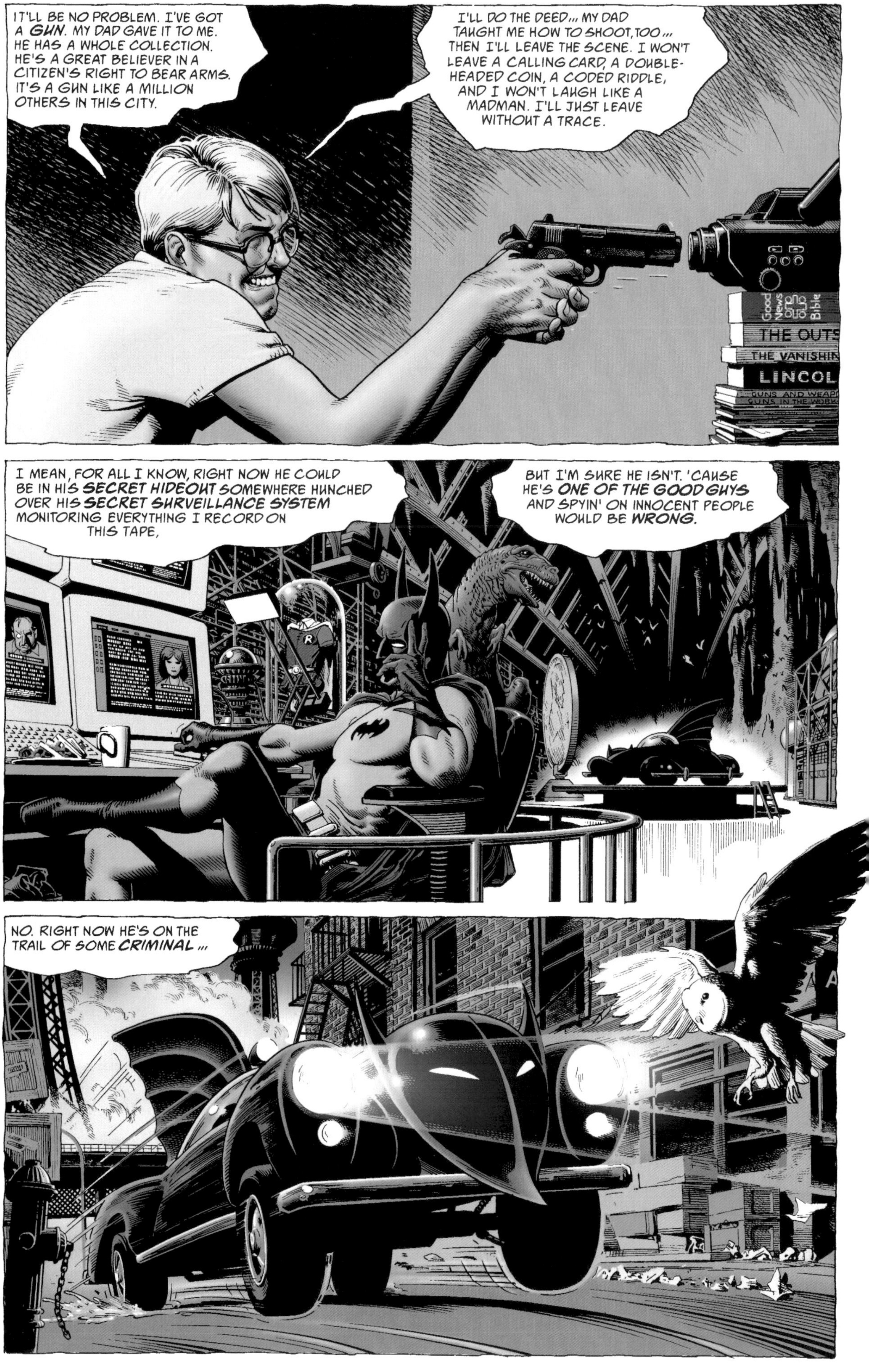
IT'LL BE NO PROBLEM. I'VE GOT A GUN. MY DAD GAVE IT TO ME. HE HAS A WHOLE COLLECTION. HE'S A GREAT BELIEVER IN A CITIZEN'S RIGHT TO BEAR ARMS. IT'S A GUN LIKE A MILLION OTHERS IN THIS CITY.
I'LL DO THE DEED... MY DAD TAUGHT ME HOW TO SHOOT, TOO... THEN I'LL LEAVE THE SCENE. I WON'T LEAVE A CALLING CARD, A DOUBLE-HEADED COIN, A CODED RIDDLE, AND I WON'T LAUGH LIKE A MADMAN. I'LL JUST LEAVE WITHOUT A TRACE.
I MEAN, FOR ALL I KNOW, RIGHT NOW HE COULD BE IN HIS SECRET HIDEOUT SOMEWHERE HUNCHED OVER HIS SECRET SURVEILLANCE SYSTEM MONITORING EVERYTHING I RECORD ON THIS TAPE,
BUT I'M SURE HE ISN'T. 'CAUSE HE'S ONE OF THE GOOD GUYS AND SPYIN' ON INNOCENT PEOPLE WOULD BE WRONG.
NO. RIGHT NOW HE'S ON THE TRAIL OF SOME CRIMINAL...

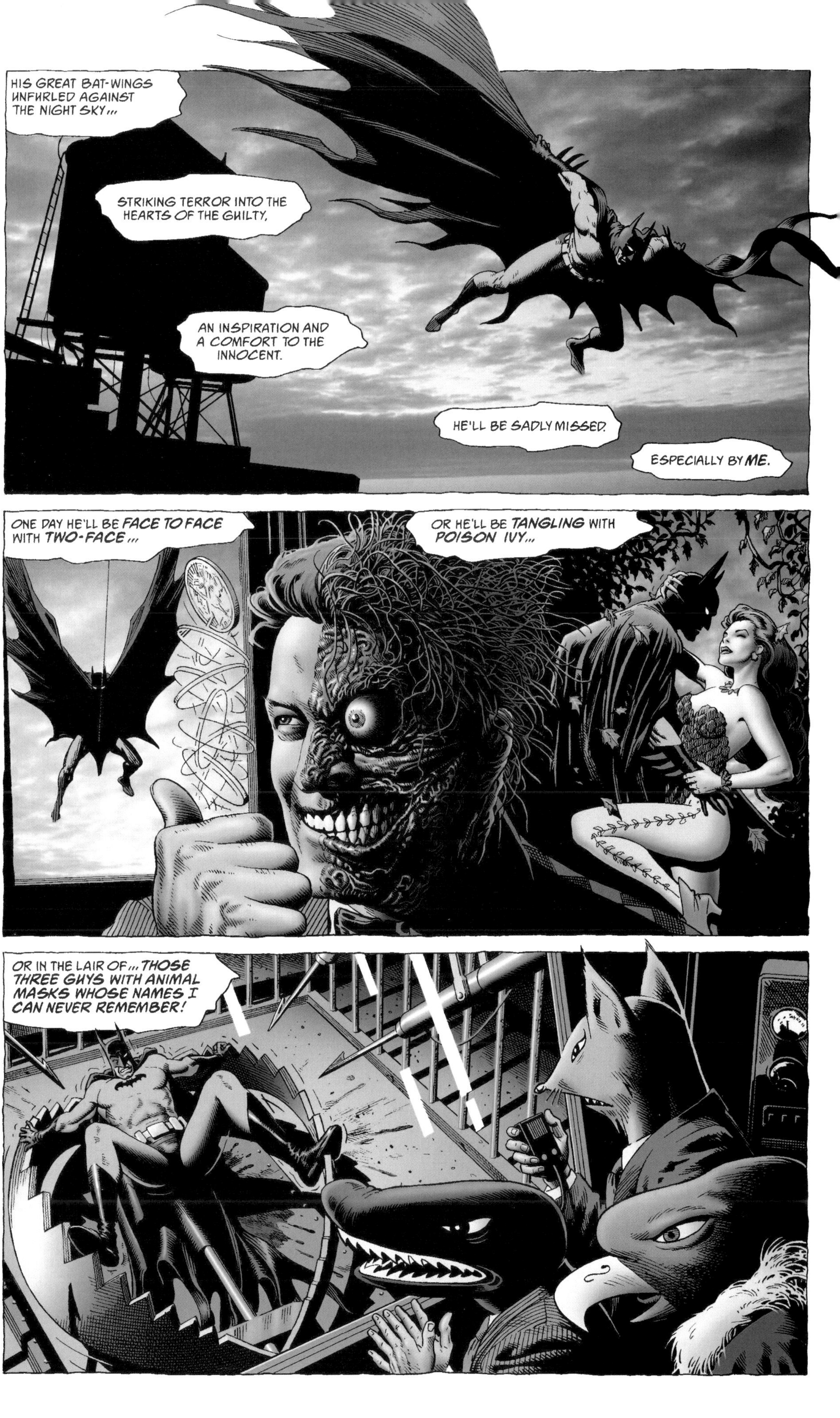
HIS GREAT BAT-WINGS UNFURLED AGAINST THE NIGHT SKY...
STRIKING TERROR INTO THE HEARTS OF THE GUILTY,
AN INSPIRATION AND A COMFORT TO THE INNOCENT.
HE'LL BE SADLY MISSED.
ESPECIALLY BY ME.
ONE DAY HE'LL BE FACE TO FACE WITH TWO-FACE...
OR HE'LL BE TANGLING WITH POISON IVY...
OR IN THE LAIR OF... THOSE THREE GUYS WITH ANIMAL MASKS WHOSE NAMES I CAN NEVER REMEMBER!

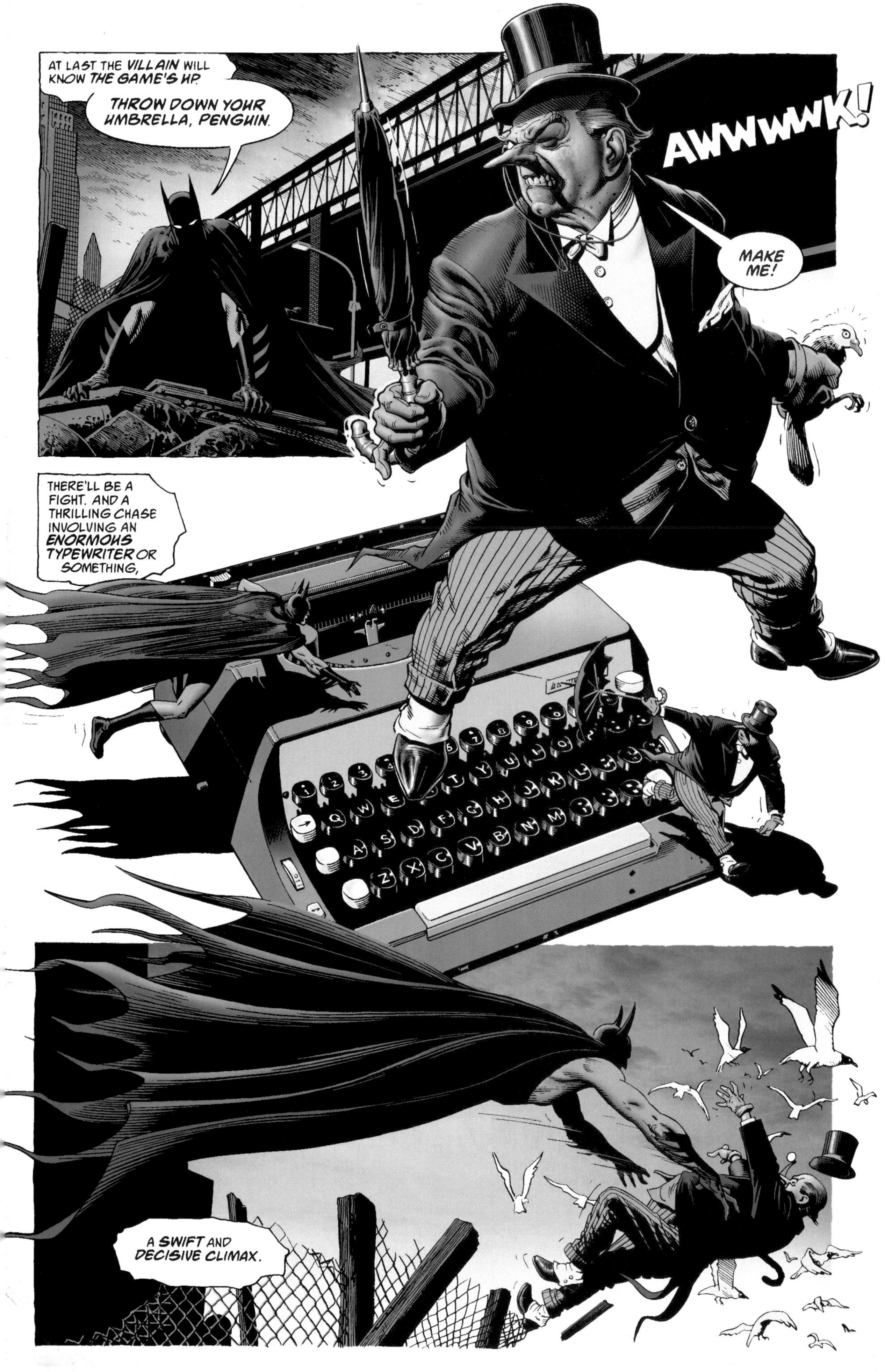
AT LAST THE VILLAIN WILL KNOW THE GAME'S UP.
THROW DOWN YOUR UMBRELLA, PENGUIN.
AWWWWK!
MAKE ME!
THERE'LL BE A FIGHT. AND A THRILLING CHASE INVOLVING AN ENORMOUS TYPEWRITER OR SOMETHING,
A SWIFT AND DECISIVE CLIMAX.

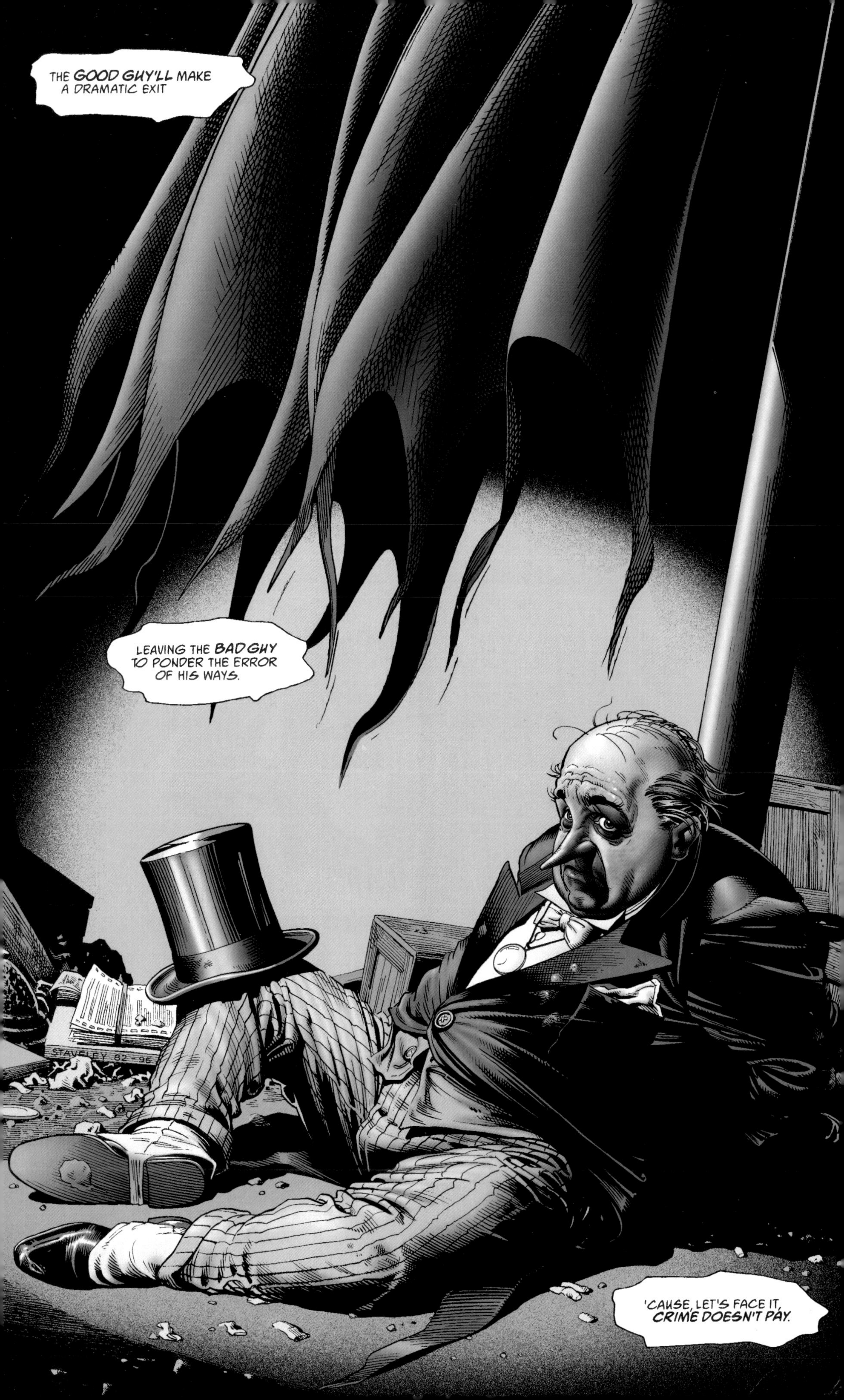
THE GOOD GUY'LL MAKE A DRAMATIC EXIT
LEAVING THE BAD GUY TO PONDER THE ERROR OF HIS WAYS.
'CAUSE, LET'S FACE IT, CRIME DOESN'T PAY.
STAVELEY 82 96

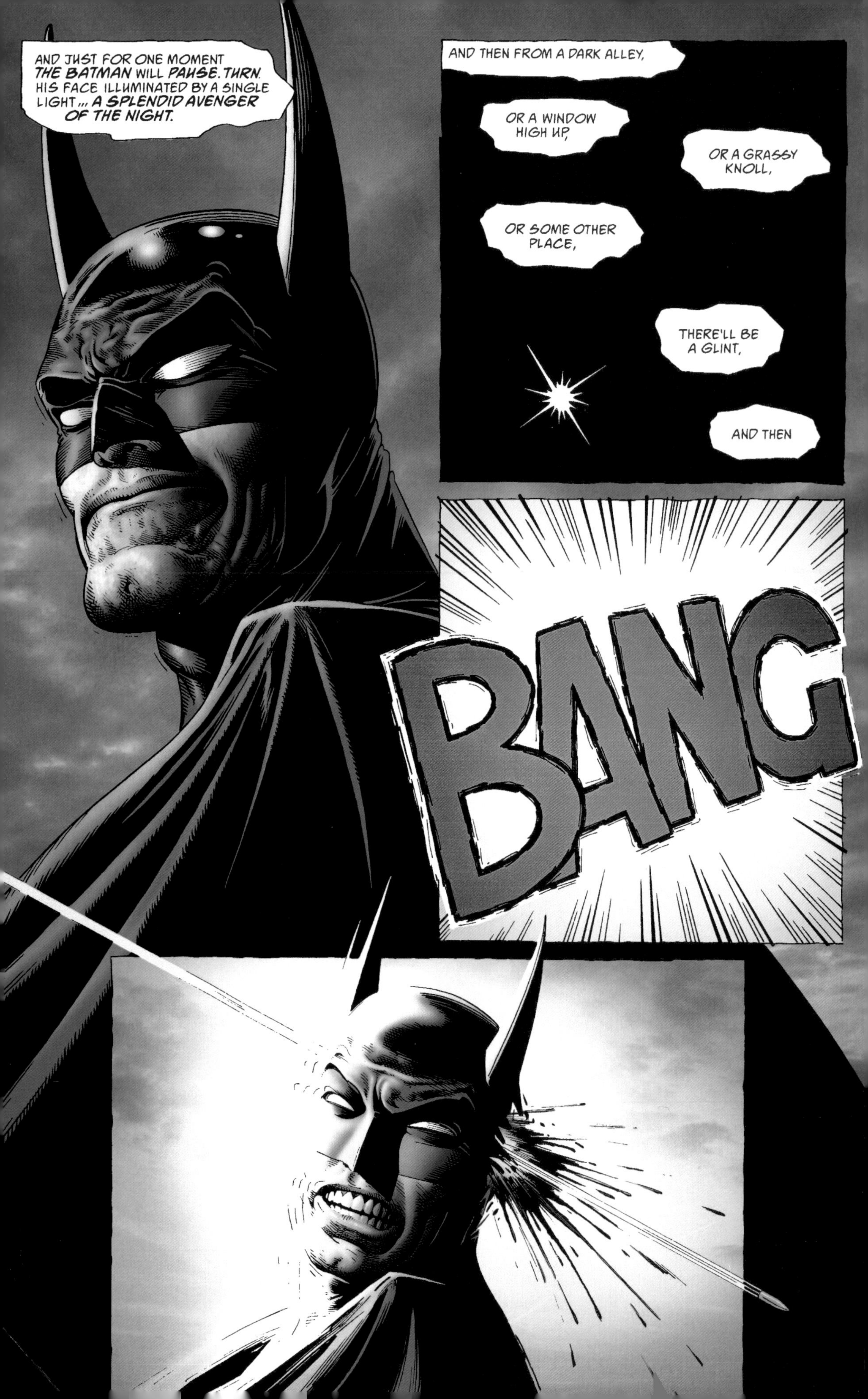
AND JUST FOR ONE MOMENT *THE BATMAN* WILL *PAUSE*. *TURN*. HIS FACE ILLUMINATED BY A SINGLE LIGHT ... *A SPLENDID AVENGER OF THE NIGHT.*
AND THEN FROM A DARK ALLEY,
OR A WINDOW HIGH UP,
OR A GRASSY KNOLL,
OR SOME OTHER PLACE,
THERE'LL BE A GLINT,
AND THEN
BANG

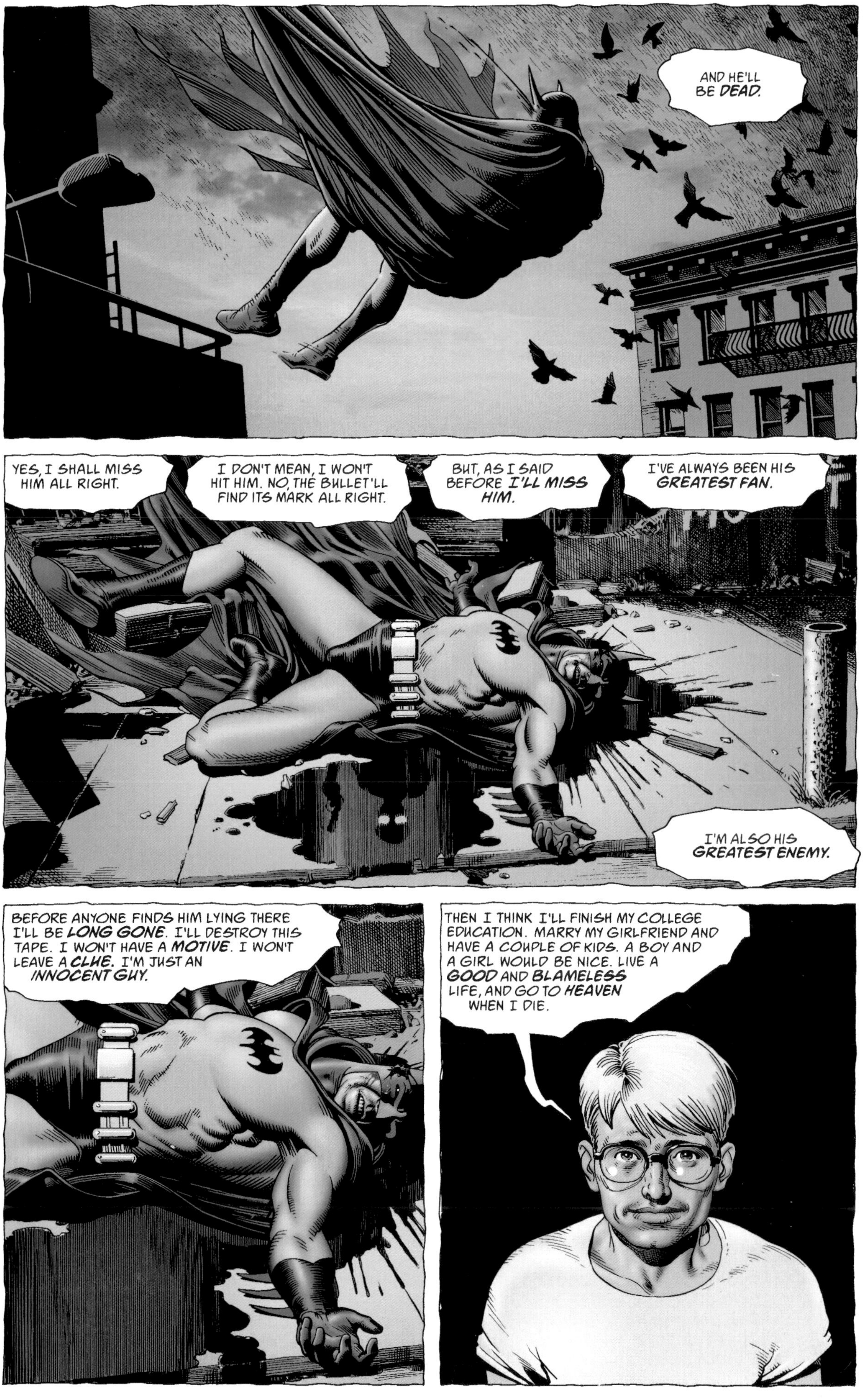

AND HE'LL BE DEAD.
YES, I SHALL MISS HIM ALL RIGHT.
I DON'T MEAN, I WON'T HIT HIM. NO, THE BULLET'LL FIND ITS MARK ALL RIGHT.
BUT, AS I SAID BEFORE I'LL MISS HIM.
I'VE ALWAYS BEEN HIS GREATEST FAN.
I'M ALSO HIS GREATEST ENEMY.
BEFORE ANYONE FINDS HIM LYING THERE I'LL BE LONG GONE. I'LL DESTROY THIS TAPE. I WON'T HAVE A MOTIVE. I WON'T LEAVE A CLUE. I'M JUST AN INNOCENT GUY.
THEN I THINK I'LL FINISH MY COLLEGE EDUCATION. MARRY MY GIRLFRIEND AND HAVE A COUPLE OF KIDS. A BOY AND A GIRL WOULD BE NICE. LIVE A GOOD AND BLAMELESS LIFE, AND GO TO HEAVEN WHEN I DIE.

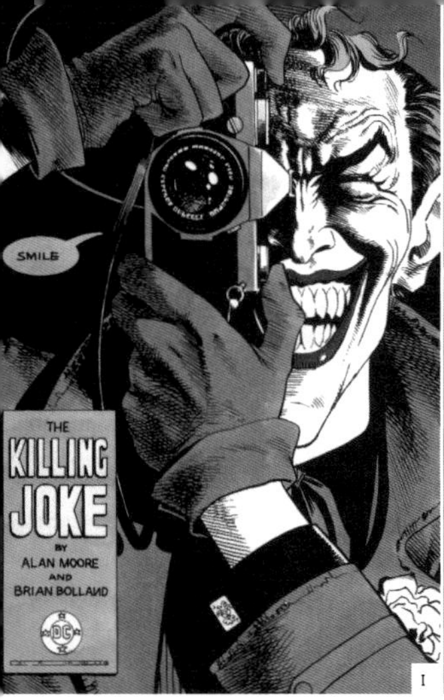
SMILE
THE KILLING JOKE
BY ALAN MOORE AND BRIAN BOLLAND

1

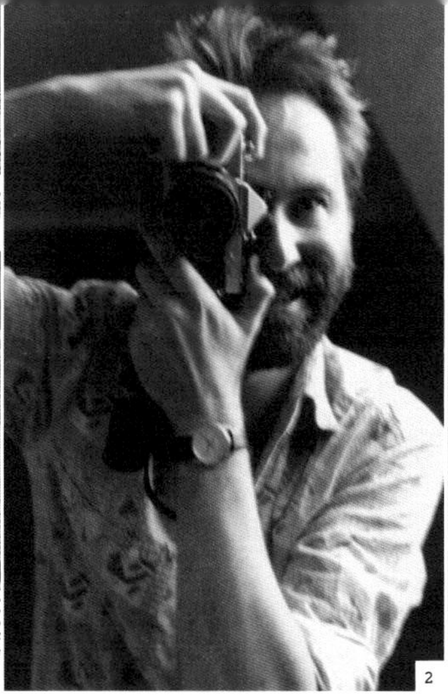

2

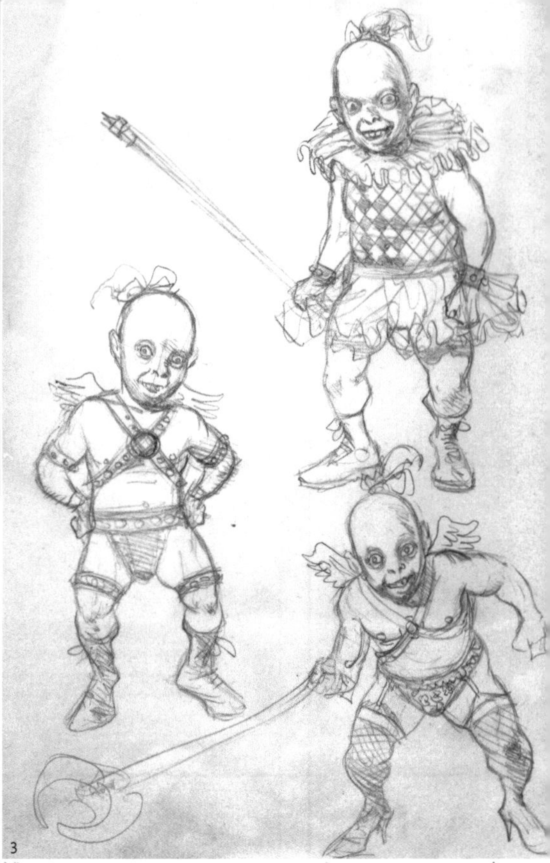

3

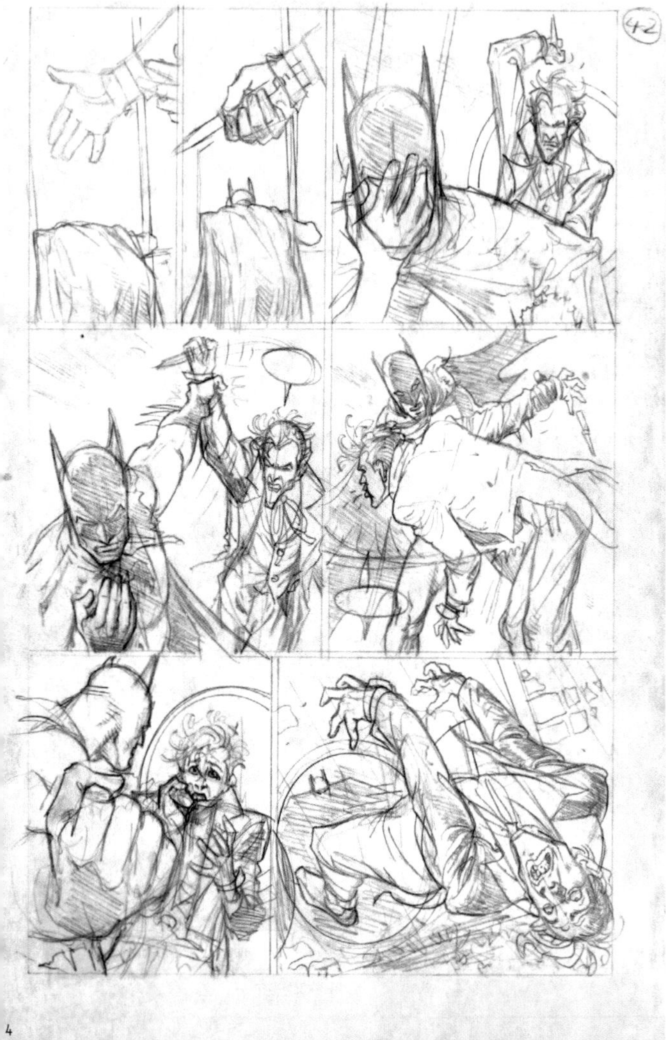
42

4

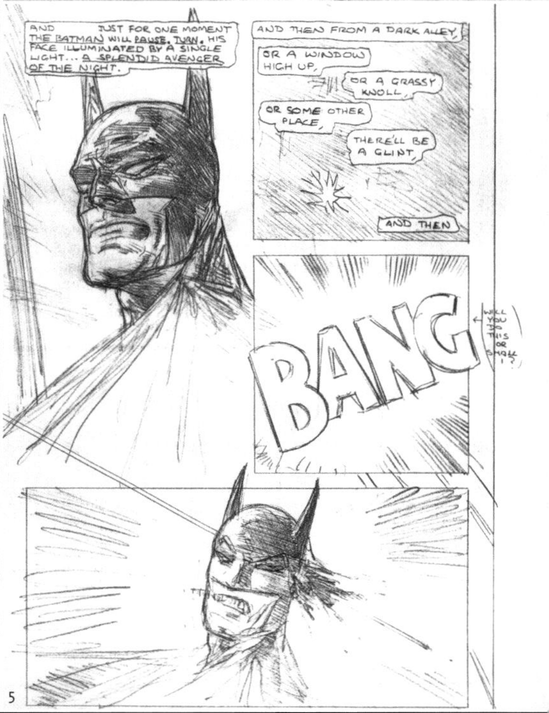
AND JUST FOR ONE MOMENT THE BATMAN WILL PAUSE, TURN. HIS FACE ILLUMINATED BY A SINGLE LIGHT... A SPLENDID AVENGER OF THE NIGHT.
AND THEN FROM A DARK ALLEY,
OR A WINDOW HIGH UP,
OR A GRASSY KNOLL,
OR SOME OTHER PLACE,
THERE'LL BE A GLINT,
AND THEN
BANG

5

From the files of Brian Bolland

Figures 1 and **2** are giving away a closely guarded professional secret. Yes, I did use photographic reference for the cover of THE KILLING JOKE! Since it's a mirror image of me in the photo you'll notice that it's actually the thumb of my left hand that's pressing the button to take the picture. The resulting sketch is probably the most thorough cover rough I've ever drawn and the only one in color. I must have been very keen to push the idea.

The evil dwarves (**figure 3**) were written into the script by Alan and given the names of three characters owned by another major company — so they can't be repeated here. I always wanted to apologize to any persons of diminutive stature who

As with the artwork, all the small "prelim" pages are now in the hands of collectors, and **figure 4** is the only one we could track down. I had more success with the *Innocent Guy* prelims. I have copies of some of them here (**figures 5,9,10**). This, incidentally, was the form in which I originally wrote the story and presented it to my editor, Mark Chiarello.

Figure 6 was drawn in Paris (with a series of markers that were running low on ink, by the looks of things) and Italian artist Tanino Liberatore produced a painted version of it for the French edition of THE KILLING JOKE. **Figures 7** and **8** are sketches of the Joker in his various guises.

WHAT'S SO FUNNY ?

IT'LL BE NO PROBLEM, I GOTTA GUN. MY DAD GAVE IT TO ME. HE'S GOT A WHOLE COLLECTION. HE'S A GREAT BELIEVER IN A CITIZEN'S RIGHT TO BEAR ARMS. ITS A GUN JUST LIKE A MILLION OTHERS IN THIS CITY.

I'LL DO THE DEED ... MY DAD TAUGHT ME HOW TO SHOOT, TOO. THEN I'LL LEAVE THE SCENE. I WON'T LEAVE A CALLING CARD, A DOUBLE-HEADED COIN, A RIDDLE AND I WON'T LAUGH LIKE A MADMAN. I'LL JUST LEAVE WITHOUT A TRACE.

8

I MEAN, FOR ALL I KNOW, RIGHT NOW HE COULD BE IN HIS SECRET HIDE-OUT SOMEWHERE HUNCHED OVER HIS SECRET SURVEILLANCE SISTEM, MONITERING EVERY-THING I RECORD ON THIS TAPE.

BUT I'M SURE HE ISN'T. 'CAUSE HE'S ONE OF THE GOOD-GUYS AND SPYIN' ON INNOCENT PEOPLE WOULD BE WRONG.

9

LEAVING THE BAD GUY TO PONDER THE ERROR OF HIS WAYS.

'CAUSE, LET'S FACE IT, CRIME DOESN'T PAY.

ALAN MOORE

Alan Moore is perhaps the most acclaimed writer in the graphic story medium, having garnered countless awards for such works as WATCHMEN, V FOR VENDETTA, *From Hell*, *Miracleman* and SWAMP THING. He is also the mastermind behind the America's Best Comics line, through which he has created (along with many talented illustrators) THE LEAGUE OF EXTRAORDINARY GENTLEMEN, PROMETHEA, TOM STRONG, TOMORROW STORIES and TOP TEN. As one of the medium's most important innovators since the early 1980s, Moore has influenced an entire generation of comics creators, and his work continues to inspire an ever-growing audience. Moore resides in central England.

BRIAN BOLLAND

After making his professional debut in 1975, Brian Bolland perfected his clean-line style and meticulous attention to detail on a series of popular strips for the British comics magazine *2000 AD*, most notably its signature feature *Judge Dredd*. He went on to illustrate the 12-issue maxiseries *CAMELOT 3000* and BATMAN: THE KILLING JOKE for DC before shifting his focus to work almost exclusively on cover illustrations. Since then, he has earned a reputation as one of the best cover artists in the industry, and his elegantly composed and beautifully rendered pieces have graced a host of titles, including ANIMAL MAN, BATMAN, THE FLASH, THE INVISIBLES, WONDER WOMAN and many more.